100

Best Slow Cooker

Dishes

100

Best Slow Cooker

Dishes

The ultimate guide to the slow cooker including 100 delicious recipes

This edition published in 2012

LOVE FOOD is an imprint of Parragon Books Ltd

Parragon

Queen Street House

4 Queen Street

Bath BA1 1HE, UK

ISBN: 978-1-4454-6195-3

Printed in China

Cover photography by Clive Streeter
Additional photography by Mike Cooper
Introduction by Linda Doeser

Notes for the Reader

This book uses standard kitchen measuring spoons and cups. All spoon
and cup measurements are level unless otherwise indicated. Unless
otherwise stated, milk is assumed to be whole, eggs are large, individual
vegetables are medium, and pepper is freshly ground black pepper.

The times given are only an approximate guide. Preparation times differ
according to the techniques used by different people and the cooking
times may also vary from those given. Optional ingredients, variations, or
serving suggestions have not been included in the calculations.

Recipes using raw or very lightly cooked eggs should be avoided by
infants, the elderly, pregnant women, and anyone with a chronic illness.
Pregnant and breast-feeding women are advised to avoid eating peanuts
and peanut products. People with nut allergies should be aware that
some of the prepared ingredients used in the recipes in this book may
contain nuts. Always check the packaging before use.

Vegetarians should be aware that some of the prepared ingredients used
in the recipes in this book may contain animal products. Always check
the packaging before use.

CONTENTS

INTRODUCTION

A wide variety of tasty, nourishing, healthy, and economical meals that are easy to prepare and don't require a lot of time and effort in the kitchen—that's what all family cooks would like. But somehow it doesn't always work that way—unless, of course, you use a slow cooker.

Also known as a crockpot, the slow cooker is a countertop electric "casserole" that cooks food with low, steady, moist heat. After vegetables have been sliced or chopped, onions softened, and meat browned, the ingredients of a delicious one-dish meal are packed into the cooking pot, then covered with the lid and the cooker turned on. These appliances are designed to cook food over a period of 8 to 12 hours, and they range in size from 1 to 6 quarts. Slow cookers can cook a dish while you're at work, and they don't heat up the kitchen. On the minus side is that some vegetables (such as celery) can become mushy before the other ingredients are done.

Because the slow cooker operates at a much lower temperature than the oven or stove, there's no risk of its contents boiling over or drying out. It's ideal for tenderizing less expensive cuts of meat and also helps the family budget by using only about as much electricity as a lightbulb. Once it has reached the optimum temperature, steam condenses on the inside of the lid, forming a seal that locks in flavor and essential vitamins and minerals, so it's both a tasty and a healthy option.

Hints & tips

• Read the manufacturer's instructions because cooker models may vary.

• Stand the cooker on a flat surface out of the reach of children and make sure that the electric cable isn't dangling.

• Thaw frozen food, especially poultry, before adding it to the slow cooker.

• If your cooker has a removable cooking pot, lift it out before adding the ingredients to avoid spills in the cooker base.

• For best results, the cooker should be filled at least halfway but never more than two-thirds full.

• Because root vegetables take a long time to cook, make sure that they are completely covered with liquid.

• Dried beans must be soaked for at least 5 hours (overnight is better), drained and rinsed, boiled in clean water for 10 minutes, then drained and rinsed again before using in a slow cooker with liquids, such as fresh water, to avoid potential food poisoning.

• Once the cooker is turned on, don't open the lid, especially in the first half of the cooking time; this breaks the condensation seal and reduces the temperature, and it takes up to 20 minutes to return to the optimum temperature.

• If leaving the cooker unattended, set the control to low. If you have an auto setting that starts on high and then automatically switches to low, you can use it instead.

• Switch off the cooker before lifting out the removable cooking pot and serving.

• Don't use the slow cooker for reheating leftovers.

1

MEAT

Traditional Pot Roast

SERVES 6

1 onion, finely chopped

4 carrots, sliced

4 baby turnips, sliced

4 celery stalks, sliced

2 potatoes, sliced

1 sweet potato, sliced

3–4 pounds bottom round roast
  or rump roast

1 bouquet garni (sprigs of parsley,
  bay leaf, and thyme tied together)

1¼ cups hot beef stock

salt and pepper

Method

1 Place the onion, carrots, turnips, celery, potatoes, and sweet potato in the slow cooker and stir to mix well.

2 Rub the beef all over with salt and pepper, then place on top of the bed of vegetables. Add the bouquet garni and pour in the stock. Cover and cook on low for 9–10 hours, until the beef is cooked to your liking. Remove and discard the bouquet garni, and serve immediately.

02

Traditional Beef Stew

SERVES 6

1/4 cup all-purpose flour

2 1/4 pounds chuck steak, cut into
   1 1/2-inch cubes

2 tablespoons sunflower oil

3 ounces bacon, diced

4 tablespoons (1/2 stick) salted butter

2 onions, thinly sliced

4 carrots, sliced

5 potatoes, cut into chunks

1 1/2 cups sliced white button
   mushrooms

1 bay leaf

2 fresh thyme sprigs, finely chopped,
   plus extra sprigs to garnish

1 tablespoon finely chopped fresh
   parsley

14 1/2-ounce can diced tomatoes

1 1/2 cups beef stock

salt and pepper

Method

1 Put the flour into a plastic food bag and season to taste with salt and pepper. Add the steak cubes, in batches, hold the top securely, and shake well to coat. Transfer the meat to a plate.

2 Heat the oil in a large skillet. Add the bacon and cook over low heat, stirring frequently, for 5 minutes. Add the steak cubes, increase the heat to medium, and cook, stirring frequently, for 8–10 minutes, until evenly browned. Remove the meat with a slotted spoon and set aside on a plate.

3 Wipe out the skillet with paper towels, then return to low heat and melt the butter. Add the onions and cook, stirring occasionally, for 5 minutes, until softened. Add the carrots, potatoes, and mushrooms and cook, stirring occasionally, for an additional 5 minutes.

4 Season to taste with salt and pepper, add the bay leaf, chopped thyme, parsley, and tomatoes, and pour in the stock. Bring to a boil, stirring occasionally, then remove the skillet from the heat and transfer the mixture to the slow cooker. Stir in the meat, cover, and cook on low for 8–9 hours. Remove and discard the bay leaf. Garnish with thyme sprigs and serve immediately.

Beef in Beer

SERVES 4–6

1/4 cup sunflower oil

2 1/4 pounds bottom round roast or rump roast

3 1/4 pounds red onions, thinly sliced

2 cups beef stock

1 1/2 tablespoons all-purpose flour

1 1/2 cups beer

3 garlic cloves, chopped

1 strip thinly pared lemon rind

1 bay leaf

2 tablespoons molasses

salt and pepper

fresh flat-leaf parsley sprigs, to garnish

Method

1 Heat the oil in a large skillet. Add the beef and cook over medium–high heat, turning occasionally, for 5–8 minutes, until evenly browned. Transfer the beef to the slow cooker.

2 Reduce the heat to low and add the onions to the skillet. Cook, stirring occasionally, for 5 minutes, until softened. Stir in 2 tablespoons of the stock, scraping up the sediment from the bottom of the skillet, and cook until all the liquid has evaporated. Add another 2 tablespoons of the stock and continue to cook for an additional 15 minutes, adding 2 tablespoons of the stock each time the previous addition has evaporated.

3 Stir in the flour and cook, stirring continuously, for 1 minute, then gradually stir in the remaining stock and the beer. Increase the heat to medium and bring to a boil, stirring continuously.

4 Stir in the garlic, lemon rind, bay leaf, and molasses and season to taste with salt and pepper. Transfer the onion mixture to the slow cooker, cover, and cook on low for 8–9 hours, until the beef is cooked to your liking. Serve immediately, garnished with parsley sprigs.

Pot Roast with Beer

SERVES 4–6

2 small onions, each cut into
   8 wedges

8 small carrots, halved lengthwise

1 fennel bulb, cut into 8 wedges

5 pounds rolled chuck steak

2 tablespoons Dijon mustard

1 tablespoon all-purpose flour

1/2 cup beer

salt and pepper

Method

1 Place the onions, carrots, and fennel in the slow cooker and season to taste with salt and pepper. Place the beef on top.

2 Mix the mustard and flour together to form a paste and spread it over the beef. Season well and pour over the beer. Cover and cook on low for 8 hours.

3 Remove the beef and vegetables with a slotted spoon and transfer to a warm serving plate. Skim the excess fat from the juices and pour the juices into a pitcher to serve with the beef. Serve immediately.

05

Hungarian Goulash

SERVES 4

1/4 cup sunflower oil

1 1/2 pounds chuck steak,
   cut into 1-inch cubes

2 teaspoons all-purpose flour

2 teaspoons paprika

1 1/4 cups beef stock

3 onions, chopped

4 carrots, diced

1 large potato or 2 medium
   potatoes, diced

1 bay leaf

1/2–1 teaspoon caraway seeds

14 1/2-ounce can diced tomatoes

2 tablespoons sour cream

salt and pepper

Method

1 Heat half of the oil in a heavy skillet. Add the beef and cook over medium heat, stirring frequently, until evenly browned. Reduce the heat and stir in the flour and paprika. Cook, stirring continuously, for 2 minutes. Gradually stir in the stock and bring to a boil, then transfer the mixture to the slow cooker.

2 Wipe out the pan with paper towels, then heat the remaining oil. Add the onions and cook over low heat, stirring occasionally, for 5 minutes, until softened. Stir in the carrots and potato and cook for an additional few minutes. Add the bay leaf, caraway seeds, and tomatoes. Season to taste with salt and pepper.

3 Transfer the vegetable mixture to the slow cooker and stir well, then cover and cook on low for 9 hours, until the meat is tender.

4 Remove and discard the bay leaf. Stir in the sour cream and transfer to warm serving plates. Serve immediately.

06

Beef Bourguignon

SERVES 6

2 tablespoons all-purpose flour

2 pounds chuck steak, trimmed and cut into 1-inch cubes

6 bacon strips, chopped

3 tablespoons olive oil

2 tablespoons unsalted butter

12 pearl onions or shallots

2 garlic cloves, finely chopped

2/3 cup beef stock

2 cups full-bodied red wine

1 bouquet garni (sprigs of parsley, bay leaf, and thyme tied together)

2 cups quartered white button mushrooms

salt and pepper

Method

1 Put the flour into a plastic food bag and season to taste with salt and pepper. Add the steak cubes, in batches, hold the top securely, and shake well to coat. Transfer the meat to a plate.

2 Cook the bacon in a large, heavy saucepan, stirring occasionally, until the fat runs and the bacon is crisp. Using a slotted spoon, transfer the bacon to a plate. Add the oil to the saucepan. When it is hot, add the steak cubes and cook, in batches, stirring occasionally, for 5 minutes, until evenly browned. Transfer to the plate with a slotted spoon.

3 Add the butter to the saucepan. When it has melted, add the onions and garlic and cook, stirring occasionally, for 5 minutes. Return the bacon and steak to the pan and pour in the stock and wine. Bring to a boil.

4 Transfer the mixture to the slow cooker and add the bouquet garni. Cover and cook on low for 7 hours, until the meat is tender.

5 Add the mushrooms to the slow cooker and stir well. Re-cover and cook on high for 15 minutes.

6 Remove and discard the bouquet garni. Taste and adjust the seasoning, adding salt and pepper if needed. Transfer to warm serving bowls and serve immediately.

07

Tagliatelle with Meat Sauce

SERVES 6

3 tablespoons olive oil

3 ounces pancetta or bacon, diced

1 onion, chopped

1 garlic clove, finely chopped

1 carrot, chopped

1 celery stalk, chopped

1 pound ground beef

1/2 cup red wine

2 tablespoons tomato paste

14 1/2-ounce can diced tomatoes

1 1/4 cups beef stock

1/2 teaspoon dried oregano

1 bay leaf

1 pound dried tagliatelle

salt and pepper

grated Parmesan cheese, to serve

Method

1 Heat the oil in a saucepan. Add the pancetta and cook over medium heat, stirring frequently, for 3 minutes. Reduce the heat, add the onion, garlic, carrot, and celery and cook, stirring occasionally, for 5 minutes, until the vegetables have softened.

2 Increase the heat to medium and add the ground beef. Cook, stirring frequently and breaking it up with a wooden spoon, for 8–10 minutes, until evenly browned. Pour in the wine and cook for a few minutes, until the alcohol has evaporated, then stir in the tomato paste, tomatoes, stock, oregano, and bay leaf and season to taste with salt and pepper.

3 Bring to a boil, then transfer the meat sauce to the slow cooker. Cover and cook on low for 8–8 1/2 hours.

4 Shortly before serving, bring a large saucepan of salted water to a boil. Add the pasta, bring back to a boil and cook for 8–10 minutes, or according to the package directions, until tender but still firm to the bite. Drain and transfer to a warm serving bowl. Remove and discard the bay leaf, then add the meat sauce to the pasta. Toss with two forks, sprinkle with the Parmesan, and serve immediately.

08

Beef & Chipotle Burritos

SERVES 4

1 tablespoon olive oil

1 onion, sliced

1¼ pounds chuck steak

1 dried chipotle pepper, soaked in boiling water for 20 minutes

1 garlic clove, crushed

1 teaspoon ground cumin

14¼-ounce can diced tomatoes

8 tortillas

salt and pepper

sour cream and green salad, to serve

Method

1 Heat the oil in a saucepan and sauté the onion for 3–4 minutes, until golden. Transfer to the slow cooker and arrange the beef on top. Drain and chop the chipotle. Sprinkle over the meat with the garlic, cumin, tomatoes, salt and pepper.

2 Cover and cook on low for 4 hours, until the meat is tender.

3 Warm the tortillas. Remove the beef and shred with a fork. Divide among the tortillas and spoon over the sauce. Wrap, and serve with sour cream and green salad.

09

Chunky Beef Chili

SERVES 4

2 1/2 cups dried red kidney beans, soaked overnight or for at least 5 hours, drained, and rinsed

2 1/2 cups cold water

2 garlic cloves, chopped

1/3 cup tomato paste

1 small green chile, chopped

2 teaspoons ground cumin

2 teaspoons ground coriander

1 1/4 pounds chuck steak, diced

1 large onion, chopped

1 large green bell pepper, seeded and sliced

salt and pepper

sour cream, to serve

Method

1 Put the kidney beans into a saucepan, cover with cold water, and bring to a boil. Boil rapidly for 10 minutes and remove from the heat, then drain and rinse again. Place the beans in the slow cooker and add the cold water.

2 Mix together the garlic, tomato paste, chile, cumin, and coriander in a large bowl. Add the steak, onion, and green bell pepper and mix to coat evenly.

3 Place the meat and vegetables on top of the beans, cover, and cook on low for 9 hours, until the beans and meat are tender. Stir and season to taste with salt and pepper.

4 Transfer to warm serving bowls and top with a swirl of sour cream. Serve immediately.

10

Italian Slow Braised Beef

SERVES 6

1 1/4 cups red wine

1/4 cup olive oil

1 celery stalk, chopped

2 shallots, sliced

4 garlic cloves, finely chopped

1 bay leaf

10 fresh basil leaves, plus extra
   to garnish

3 fresh parsley sprigs

pinch of grated nutmeg

pinch of ground cinnamon

2 cloves

3 1/4 pounds bottom round roast or
   rump roast

1–2 garlic cloves, thinly sliced

2 ounces bacon or pancetta,
   chopped

14 1/2-ounce can diced tomatoes

2 tablespoons tomato paste

Method

1 Combine the wine, half of the oil, the celery, shallots, garlic, herbs, and spices in a large nonmetallic bowl. Add the beef, cover, and let marinate, turning occasionally, for 12 hours.

2 Drain the beef, reserving the marinade, and pat dry with paper towels. Make small incisions all over the beef using a sharp knife. Insert a slice of garlic and a piece of bacon in each "pocket." Heat the remaining oil in a large skillet. Add the meat and cook over medium heat, turning frequently, until evenly browned. Transfer to the slow cooker.

3 Strain the reserved marinade into the skillet and bring to a boil. Stir in the tomatoes and tomato paste. Stir well, then pour the mixture over the beef. Cover and cook on low for about 8–9 hours, until the beef is cooked to your liking. If possible, turn the beef over halfway through the cooking time.

4 Remove the beef from the slow cooker and place on a carving board. Cover with aluminum foil and let rest for 10–15 minutes until firm. Cut into slices and transfer to a serving plate. Spoon over the sauce, garnish with basil leaves, and serve immediately.

11

Caribbean Beef Stew

SERVES 6

1 pound chuck steak

3½ cups diced butternut or acorn squash

1 onion, chopped

1 red bell pepper, seeded and chopped

2 garlic cloves, finely chopped

1-inch-piece fresh ginger, finely chopped

1 tablespoon sweet or hot paprika

1 cup beef stock

14½-ounce can diced tomatoes

15–16-ounce can pigeon peas or chickpeas (garbanzo beans), drained and rinsed

15–16-ounce can black-eyed peas, drained and rinsed

salt and pepper

Method

1 Trim off any visible fat from the steak, then dice the meat. Heat a large, heavy saucepan without adding any extra fat. Add the meat and cook, stirring continuously, for a few minutes, until evenly browned. Stir in the squash, onion, and red bell pepper and cook for 1 minute, then add the garlic, ginger, and paprika. Pour in the stock and tomatoes and bring to a boil.

2 Transfer the mixture to the slow cooker, cover, and cook on low for 7 hours. Add the pigeon peas and black-eyed peas to the stew and season to taste with salt and pepper. Re-cover and cook on high for 30 minutes. Transfer to warm serving bowls and serve immediately.

12

Beef in Coffee Sauce

SERVES 6

1/4 cup sunflower oil

3 pounds chuck steak,
  cut into 1-inch cubes

4 onions, sliced

1 garlic clove, finely chopped

1/3 cup all-purpose flour

1 1/4 cups red wine

pinch of dried oregano

1 small fresh rosemary sprig

2 cups black coffee

salt and pepper

fresh marjoram sprigs, to garnish

mashed sweet potatoes, to serve

Method

1 Heat the oil in a large skillet. Add the steak cubes and cook over medium heat, stirring frequently, for 8–10 minutes, until evenly browned. Transfer to the slow cooker with a slotted spoon.

2 Add the onions and garlic to the skillet, reduce the heat, and cook, stirring occasionally, for 10 minutes, until softened and just beginning to color. Stir in the flour and cook, stirring continuously, for 1 minute. Gradually stir in the wine, a little at a time. Add the oregano and rosemary, season to taste with salt and pepper, pour in the coffee, and bring to a boil, stirring continuously.

3 Transfer the mixture to the slow cooker. Cover and cook on low for 8–9 hours, until the meat is tender. Remove and discard the rosemary sprig. Taste and adjust the seasoning, adding salt and pepper if needed. Transfer to warm serving plates, garnish with marjoram sprigs and serve immediately with mashed sweet potatoes.

13

Beef Casserole

SERVES 6

3 tablespoons olive oil

2 1/4 pounds beef cut into
   1 1/4-inch cubes

2 onions, thinly sliced

2 garlic cloves, chopped

1 1/2 cups beef stock

2 tablespoons all-purpose flour

1/2 cup port

2 tablespoons red-currant jelly

6 juniper berries, crushed,
   or 1 tablespoon gin

4 cloves, crushed

pinch of ground cinnamon

pinch of freshly grated nutmeg

salt and pepper

chopped fresh flat-leaf parsley,
   to garnish

mashed potatoes, to serve

Method

1 Heat the oil in a heavy skillet. Add the beef and cook over high heat, stirring frequently, for 5 minutes, until browned all over. Using a slotted spoon, transfer the meat to the slow cooker.

2 Add the onions and garlic to the skillet, reduce the heat, and cook, stirring occasionally, for 5 minutes, until softened. Transfer them to the slow cooker.

3 Gradually stir the stock into the skillet, scraping up any sediment from the bottom, then bring to a boil, stirring continuously. Sprinkle the flour over the meat in the slow cooker and stir well to coat evenly. Stir in the hot stock, then stir in the port, red-currant jelly, juniper berries, cloves, cinnamon, and nutmeg. Season to taste with salt and pepper. Cover and cook on low for 7–8 hours, until the meat is tender.

4 Taste and adjust the seasoning, adding salt and pepper if needed. Remove and discard the cloves. Garnish with parsley and serve immediately with mashed potatoes.

14

Lamb with Spring Vegetables

SERVES 4–6

1/3 cup olive oil

6 shallots, chopped

1 garlic clove, chopped

2 celery stalks, chopped

2 tablespoons all-purpose flour

1 1/2 pounds boned leg or shoulder of lamb, cut into 1-inch cubes

3 1/2 cups chicken stock

1/2 cup pearled barley, rinsed

4 small turnips, halved

15 baby carrots

1 1/2 cups frozen young green peas, thawed

1 1/2 cups frozen baby fava beans, thawed

salt and pepper

chopped fresh parsley, to garnish

Method

1 Heat 3 tablespoons of the oil in a large saucepan. Add the shallots, garlic, and celery and cook over low heat, stirring occasionally, for 8–10 minutes, until softened and lightly browned.

2 Meanwhile, put the flour into a plastic food bag and season well with salt and pepper. Add the lamb cubes, in batches, hold the top securely, and shake well to coat. Transfer the meat to a plate.

3 Using a slotted spoon, transfer the softened vegetables to the slow cooker. Add the remaining oil to the pan and heat. Add the lamb, in batches if necessary, increase the heat to medium, and cook, stirring frequently, for 8–10 minutes, until evenly browned.

4 Return all the lamb to the pan. Gradually stir in the stock, scraping up the sediment from the bottom of the pan. Stir in the pearled barley, turnips, and carrots, season to taste with salt and pepper, and bring to a boil. Transfer the mixture to the slow cooker and stir well. Cover and cook on low for 8–10 hours, until the lamb is tender.

5 Add the green peas and fava beans to the slow cooker, sprinkling them evenly on top of the stew. Re-cover and cook on low for an additional 30 minutes, until heated through. Stir well, then taste and adjust the seasoning, adding salt and pepper if needed. Garnish with parsley and serve immediately.

15

Lamb Stew

SERVES 6

1¼ cups dry white wine

3 tablespoons brandy

1 tablespoon olive oil

1 fresh rosemary sprig

1 bay leaf

1 tablespoon chopped fresh parsley

2 cloves

6 allspice berries

6 black peppercorns

1 strip thinly pared orange rind

4 shallots, sliced

2 carrots, sliced

2 garlic cloves, finely chopped

3 pounds diced lamb

1 cup all-purpose flour

4 bacon strips, cut into
    1-inch pieces

2 onions, chopped

2 cups beef stock

salt and pepper

crusty bread, to serve

Method

1 Put the wine, brandy, oil, rosemary, bay leaf, parsley, cloves, allspice berries, peppercorns, orange rind, shallots, carrots, garlic, and lamb into a large nonmetallic bowl and mix well. Cover with plastic wrap and let marinate overnight in the refrigerator.

2 Drain the lamb cubes, reserving the marinade. Pat the lamb dry with paper towels. Put the flour into a plastic food bag and season to taste with salt and pepper. Add the lamb cubes, in batches, hold the top securely, and shake well to coat. Transfer the meat to a plate.

3 Cook the bacon in a large nonstick or heavy saucepan over medium heat for 3 minutes. Add the onions, reduce the heat, and cook, stirring occasionally, for 5 minutes, until softened. Add the lamb, increase the heat to medium, and cook, stirring frequently, for 8–10 minutes, until evenly browned. Pour in the reserved marinade and the stock and bring to a boil, stirring occasionally.

4 Transfer the mixture to the slow cooker, cover, and cook on low for 8–9 hours, until the meat is tender. Skim off any fat from the surface and remove and discard the rosemary, bay leaf, and orange rind. Taste and adjust the seasoning if necessary. Transfer to warm serving plates and serve immediately with crusty bread.

16

Moroccan Lamb Stew

SERVES 6

3 tablespoons olive oil

2 red onions, chopped

2 garlic cloves, finely chopped

1-inch-piece fresh ginger, finely chopped

1 yellow bell pepper, seeded and chopped

2¼ pounds boneless shoulder of lamb, trimmed and cut into 1-inch cubes

3½ cups lamb stock or chicken stock

1¾ cups dried apricots halves

1 tablespoon honey

¼ cup lemon juice

pinch of saffron threads

2-inch cinnamon stick

salt and pepper

toasted slivered almonds and fresh cilantro sprigs, to garnish

Method

1 Heat the oil in a large, heavy saucepan. Add the onions, garlic, ginger and yellow bell pepper and cook over low heat, stirring occasionally, for 5 minutes, until the onion has softened. Add the lamb and stir well to mix, then pour in the stock. Add the apricots, honey, lemon juice, saffron, and cinnamon stick and season to taste with salt and pepper. Bring to a boil.

2 Transfer the mixture to the slow cooker. Cover and cook on low for 8½ hours, until the meat is tender.

3 Remove and discard the cinnamon stick. Transfer to warm serving bowls and garnish with slivered almonds and cilantro sprigs. Serve immediately.

17

Lamb Shanks with Olives

SERVES 4

1½ tablespoons all-purpose flour

4 lamb shanks

2 tablespoons olive oil

1 onion, sliced

2 garlic cloves, finely chopped

2 teaspoons sweet paprika

14½-ounce can diced tomatoes

2 tablespoons tomato paste

2 carrots, sliced

2 teaspoons sugar

1 cup red wine

2-inch cinnamon stick

2 fresh rosemary sprigs

1 cup pitted black ripe olives

2 tablespoons lemon juice

2 tablespoons chopped fresh mint, plus extra leaves to garnish

salt and pepper

Method

1 Put the flour into a plastic food bag and season to taste with salt and pepper. Add the lamb shanks, hold the top securely, and shake well to coat.

2 Heat the oil in a large, heavy saucepan. Add the lamb shanks and cook over medium heat, turning frequently, for 6–8 minutes, until evenly browned. Transfer to a plate and set aside.

3 Add the onion and garlic to the saucepan and cook, stirring frequently, for 5 minutes, until softened. Stir in the paprika and cook for 1 minute. Add the tomatoes, tomato paste, carrots, sugar, wine, cinnamon stick, and rosemary and bring to a boil.

4 Transfer the mixture to the slow cooker and add the lamb shanks. Cover and cook on low for 8 hours, until the lamb is tender.

5 Add the olives, lemon juice, and chopped mint to the slow cooker. Re-cover and cook on high for 30 minutes. Remove and discard the rosemary and cinnamon stick. Transfer to warm serving plates, garnish with mint leaves, and serve immediately.

18

Cured Ham in Dry Cider

SERVES 6

2¼ pounds boneless cured ham

1 onion, halved

4 cloves

6 black peppercorns

1 teaspoon juniper berries

1 celery stalk, chopped

1 carrot, sliced

4¼ cups medium dry cider

fresh salad, to serve

Method

1 Place a trivet or rack in the slow cooker, if you like, and stand the ham on it. Otherwise, just place the ham in the slow cooker. Stud each onion half with two of the cloves and add to the slow cooker with the peppercorns, juniper berries, celery, and carrot.

2 Pour in the cider, cover, and cook on low for 8 hours, until the meat is tender.

3 Remove the ham from the cooker and place on a board. Tent with aluminum foil and let rest for 10–15 minutes. Discard the cooking liquid and flavorings.

4 Cut off any rind and fat from the ham and carve into slices. Transfer to serving plates and serve immediately with a fresh salad.

19

Pork with Apple & Herbs

SERVES 6

2 tablespoons all-purpose flour

1³/4 pounds boneless pork,
cut into 1-inch cubes

1/3 cup sunflower oil

1 large onion, chopped

2 garlic cloves, finely chopped

2 apples, such as Red Delicious or
McIntosh, cored and cut into
wedges

1¹/4 cups hard dry cider or
apple juice

2¹/2 cups chicken stock

2 bay leaves

2 fresh sage sprigs

1 fresh rosemary sprig

3 tablespoons chopped fresh parsley

salt and pepper

mashed potatoes, to serve

Method

1 Put the flour into a plastic food bag and season to taste with salt and pepper. Add the pork cubes, in batches, hold the top securely, and shake well to coat. Transfer the meat to a plate.

2 Heat 3 tablespoons of the oil in a large skillet. Add the pork cubes, in batches if necessary, and cook over medium heat, stirring frequently, for 5–8 minutes, until evenly browned. Transfer to a plate and set aside.

3 Add the remaining oil to the pan and heat. Add the onion and garlic and cook over low heat, stirring occasionally, for 10 minutes, until softened and lightly browned. Add the apple wedges and cook, stirring occasionally, for 3–5 minutes, until beginning to color. Gradually stir in the cider and stock, scraping up any sediment from the bottom of the skillet, and bring to a boil. Season to taste with salt and pepper, add the bay leaves, sage, and rosemary, and transfer to the slow cooker. Stir in the pork, cover, and cook on low for 6–7 hours.

4 Remove and discard the bay leaves, sage, and rosemary sprigs. Transfer the stew to warm individual plates and sprinkle with the parsley. Serve immediately with mashed potatoes.

20

Pork with Peppers & Apricots

SERVES 4

2 tablespoons olive oil

4 pork chops, trimmed of excess fat

1 shallot, chopped

2 garlic cloves, finely chopped

2 orange bell peppers, seeded and sliced

1 tablespoon all-purpose flour

2 1/2 cups chicken stock

1 tablespoon medium–hot Indian curry paste

1 cup dried apricots

salt and pepper

baby spinach leaves and cooked couscous, to serve

Method

1 Heat the oil in a large skillet. Add the chops and cook over medium heat for 2–4 minutes on each side, until evenly browned. Remove with tongs and put them into the slow cooker.

2 Add the shallot, garlic, and bell peppers to the skillet, reduce the heat, and cook, stirring occasionally, for 5 minutes, until softened. Stir in the flour and cook, stirring continuously, for 1 minute. Gradually stir in the stock, a little at a time, then add the curry paste and apricots. Bring to a boil, stirring occasionally.

3 Season to taste with salt and pepper and transfer the mixture to the slow cooker. Cover and cook on low for 8–9 hours, until the meat is tender. Transfer to warm serving plates and serve immediately with baby spinach and couscous.

21

Pork & Beans

SERVES 4

2 tablespoons sunflower oil

4 pork chops, trimmed of excess fat

1 onion, chopped

14½-ounce can diced tomatoes

15–16-ounce can baked beans

salted butter, for greasing, plus extra
for browning (optional)

6 potatoes, such as russets, white
rounders, or Yukon gold, thinly
sliced

2 cups hot chicken stock

salt and pepper

Method

1 Heat the oil in a skillet. Season the chops well with salt
and pepper, add to the skillet, and cook over medium heat for
2–3 minutes on each side, until evenly browned. Remove the skillet
from the heat and transfer the chops to a plate.

2 Mix together the onion, tomatoes, and beans in a bowl and
season to taste with salt and pepper.

3 Lightly grease the slow cooker pot with butter, then layer half
of the potatoes in the bottom. Cover with half of the tomato-and-
bean mixture. Put the chops on top, then add the remaining
tomato-and-bean mixture. Cover with the remaining potato slices.

4 Pour in the stock, cover, and cook on low for 8–10 hours. If
you like, you can remove the lid, dot the topping with butter, and
place the slow cooker pot under a preheated broiler to brown the
potatoes before serving.

22

Spicy Pulled Pork

SERVES 4

2 onions, sliced

3 1/2 pounds boned and rolled pork
shoulder

2 tablespoons demerara sugar or
other raw sugar

2 tablespoons Worcestershire sauce

1 tablespoon yellow mustard

2 tablespoons ketchup

1 tablespoon cider vinegar

salt and pepper

hamburger buns or ciabatta rolls,
to serve

Method

1 Put the onions in the slow cooker and place the pork on top.
Mix together the sugar, Worcestershire sauce, mustard, ketchup,
and vinegar and spread all over the surface of the pork. Season
to taste with salt and pepper. Cover and cook on low for 8 hours.

2 Remove the pork from the slow cooker and use two forks to
pull it apart into shreds.

3 Skim any excess fat from the juices and stir a little juice into
the pork. Serve in hamburger buns, with the remaining juices
for spooning over.

23

Spicy Pork Chops

SERVES 4

4 pork chops, trimmed of excess fat

2 tablespoons vegetable oil

two 8-ounce cans pineapple chunks in juice

1 red bell pepper, seeded and finely chopped

2 fresh jalapeño chiles, seeded and finely chopped

1 onion, finely chopped

1 tablespoon chopped fresh cilantro, plus extra sprigs to garnish

1/2 cup hot chicken stock

salt and pepper

flour tortillas, to serve

Method

1 Season the chops with salt and pepper to taste. Heat the oil in a large, heavy skillet. Add the chops and cook over medium heat for 2–3 minutes on each side, until lightly browned. Transfer the chops to the slow cooker. Drain the pineapples, reserving the juice, and set aside.

2 Add the red bell pepper, chiles, and onion to the skillet and cook, stirring occasionally, for 5 minutes, until the onion is softened. Transfer the mixture to the slow cooker and add the chopped cilantro, stock, and 1/2 cup of the reserved pineapple juice. Cover and cook on low for 6 hours, until the chops are tender.

3 Add the reserved pineapple to the slow cooker, re-cover, and cook on high for 15 minutes. Garnish with cilantro sprigs and serve immediately with flour tortillas.

Maple-glazed Pork Ribs

SERVES 4

1 onion, finely chopped

2 plum tomatoes, diced

3 tablespoons maple syrup

2 tablespoons soy sauce

2 teaspoons hot chili sauce

3 1/4 pounds pork ribs,
    cut into single ribs

salt and pepper

Method

1 Combine the onion, tomatoes, maple syrup, soy sauce, chili sauce, and salt and pepper to taste in a large bowl. Add the pork ribs and turn to coat evenly.

2 Arrange the ribs in the slow cooker, cover, and cook on high for 4 hours. If possible, turn the ribs halfway through the cooking time.

3 Lift out the ribs and place on a warm serving plate. Skim the excess fat from the juices and spoon the juices over the ribs to serve.

25

Sausage & Bean Stew

SERVES 4

2 tablespoons sunflower oil

2 onions, chopped

2 garlic cloves, finely chopped

4 ounces bacon, chopped

1 pound pork sausages

15–16-ounce can cannellini, red kidney, or black-eyed peas, drained and rinsed

2 tablespoons chopped fresh parsley

2/3 cup hot beef stock

4 slices French bread

1/2 cup shredded Swiss cheese

Method

1 Heat the oil in a heavy skillet. Add the onions and cook over low heat, stirring occasionally, for 5 minutes, until softened. Add the garlic, bacon, and sausages and cook, stirring and turning the sausages occasionally, for an additional 5 minutes.

2 Using a slotted spoon, transfer the mixture from the skillet to the slow cooker. Add the beans, parsley, and stock, then cover and cook on low for 6 hours.

3 Shortly before serving, preheat the broiler. Place the bread slices on the broiler rack and lightly toast on one side under the preheated broiler. Turn the slices over, sprinkle with the shredded cheese and place under the broiler until just melted.

4 Serve the casserole and cheese-topped toast immediately.

POULTRY

26

Chicken Noodle Soup

SERVES 4

1 onion, diced

2 celery stalks, diced

2 carrots, diced

2 1/4 pounds oven-ready chicken

3 cups hot chicken stock

4 ounces dried egg tagliatelle

2 tablespoons chopped fresh dill, plus extra sprigs to garnish

salt and pepper

Method

1 Place the onion, celery, and carrots in the slow cooker. Season the chicken all over with salt and pepper and place on top. Pour the stock over. Cover and cook on low for 5 hours.

2 Leaving the juices in the slow cooker, carefully lift out the chicken and remove the meat from the carcass, discarding the bones and skin. Cut the meat into bite-size pieces.

3 Skim the excess fat from the juices, then return the chicken to the slow cooker. Turn the setting to high.

4 Bring a large saucepan of lightly salted water to a boil. Add the tagliatelle, return to a boil, and cook for 5–6 minutes, or half of the amount of time given in the package directions. Drain well.

5 Add the tagliatelle and dill to the pot, stir well, cover, and cook on high for an additional 20 minutes. Garnish with the dill and serve immediately.

27

Chicken & Leek Soup

SERVES 6–8

12 pitted prunes

4 chicken parts

5 leeks, sliced

6 cups hot chicken stock
or beef stock

1 bouquet garni (sprigs of parsley,
bay leaf, and thyme tied together)

salt and pepper

Method

1 Place the prunes in a bowl and add cold water to cover. Set aside to soak while the soup is cooking.

2 Place the chicken parts and leeks in the slow cooker. Pour in the stock and add the bouquet garni. Cover and cook on low for 7 hours.

3 Remove the chicken from the cooker with a slotted spoon and cut the meat off the bones. Cut the meat into bite-size pieces and return it to the cooker. Alternatively, leave the chicken parts in the slow cooker to serve intact.

4 Drain the prunes and add them to the soup, then season to taste with salt and pepper. Re-cover and cook on high for 30 minutes.

5 Remove and discard the bouquet garni. Ladle the soup into warm bowls and serve immediately.

28

Chicken & Dumplings

SERVES 4

2 tablespoons olive oil

1 large onion, thinly sliced

2 carrots, cut into 3/4-inch chunks

2 cups cut green beans
   (1-inch pieces)

4 skinless, boneless chicken breasts

1 1/4 cups hot chicken stock

salt and pepper

Dumplings

12/3 cups all-purpose flour

2 1/2 teaspoons baking powder

3/4 teaspoon salt

1/2 cup shredded suet (available from
   butchers) or shortening

1/4 cup chopped parsley

Method

1 Heat 1 tablespoon of oil in a skillet, add the onion, and sauté over high heat for 3–4 minutes, or until golden. Place in the slow cooker with the carrots and beans.

2 Add the remaining oil to the skillet, then add the chicken breasts and sauté until golden, turning once. Arrange on top of the vegetables in a single layer, season well with salt and pepper, and pour over the stock. Cover and cook on low for 4 hours.

3 Turn the slow cooker up to high while making the dumplings. Sift the flour, baking powder, and salt into a bowl, stir in the suet and parsley, and season to taste with salt and pepper. Stir in just enough cold water to make a fairly firm dough, mixing lightly. Divide into 12 and shape into small balls.

4 Arrange the dumplings on top of the chicken, cover, and cook for 30 minutes on high. Transfer to warm serving plates and serve immediately.

29

Chicken & Apple Stew

SERVES 4

1 tablespoon olive oil

4 chicken parts, about 6 ounces each

1 onion, chopped

2 celery stalks, coarsely chopped

1 1/2 tablespoons all-purpose flour

1 1/4 cups apple juice

2/3 cup chicken stock

1 cooking apple, such as Granny
   Smith, cored and cut into quarters

2 bay leaves

1–2 teaspoons honey

1 yellow bell pepper, seeded and cut
   into chunks

salt and pepper

To garnish

1 large or 2 medium apples, such as
   Red Delicious, cored and sliced

1 tablespoon butter, melted

2 tablespoons demerara sugar or
   other raw sugar

1 tablespoon chopped fresh mint

Method

1 Heat the oil in a heavy skillet. Add the chicken and cook over medium–high heat, turning frequently, for 10 minutes, until golden brown. Transfer to the slow cooker. Add the onion and celery to the skillet and cook over low heat for 5 minutes, until softened. Sprinkle in the flour and cook for 2 minutes, then remove the skillet from the heat.

2 Gradually stir in the apple juice and stock, then return the skillet to the heat and bring to a boil. Stir in the cooking apple, bay leaves, and honey and season to taste. Pour the mixture over the chicken in the slow cooker, cover, and cook on low for 6 1/2 hours, until the chicken is tender and cooked through. Stir in the bell pepper, re-cover, and cook on high for 45 minutes.

3 About 10 minutes before serving, preheat the broiler to medium. Brush one side of the apple slices with half of the melted butter and sprinkle with half of the sugar. Cook under the preheated broiler for 2–3 minutes, until the sugar has caramelized. Turn the slices over with tongs, brush with the remaining butter, and sprinkle with the remaining sugar. Broil for an additional 2 minutes. Transfer the stew to warm plates and garnish with the caramelized apple slices and the mint. Serve immediately.

30

Chipotle Chicken Stew

SERVES 4–6

1 cup dried cannellini beans, soaked overnight or for at least 5 hours, drained, and rinsed

1 large onion, sliced

1 dried chipotle pepper, soaked for 20 minutes, then drained and finely chopped

3 1/4 pounds oven-ready chicken

1 cup hot chicken stock

14 1/2-ounce can diced tomatoes

1 teaspoon ground cumin

salt and pepper

Method

1 Put the beans into a saucepan, cover with fresh cold water, and bring to a boil. Boil rapidly for 10 minutes, remove from the heat, and drain and rinse again.

2 Transfer the beans to the slow cooker and add the onion and chipotle pepper. Place the chicken on top, pour over the stock and tomatoes with their can juices, sprinkle with cumin, and season with salt and pepper.

3 Cover and cook for 4 hours on high. Carefully remove the chicken and cut into eight pieces. Skim the excess fat from the juices and adjust the seasoning.

4 Spoon the beans into a warm serving dish, top with the chicken, and spoon the juices over. Serve immediately.

Chicken & Mushroom Stew

SERVES 4

1 tablespoon unsalted butter

2 tablespoons olive oil

4 pounds skinless chicken parts

2 red onions, sliced

2 garlic cloves, finely chopped

14½-ounce can diced tomatoes

2 tablespoons chopped fresh flat-
leaf parsley

6 fresh basil leaves, torn

1 tablespoon sun-dried tomato
paste or tomato paste

2/3 cup red wine

3 cups sliced white button
mushrooms

salt and pepper

Method

1 Heat the butter and oil in a heavy skillet. Add the chicken, in batches if necessary, and cook over medium–high heat, turning frequently, for 10 minutes, until golden brown all over. Using a slotted spoon, transfer the chicken to the slow cooker.

2 Add the onions and garlic to the skillet and cook over low heat, stirring occasionally, for 10 minutes, until golden. Add the tomatoes with their can juices, stir in the parsley, basil, tomato paste, and wine and season with salt and pepper. Bring to a boil, then pour the mixture over the chicken.

3 Cover the slow cooker and cook on low for 6½ hours. Stir in the mushrooms, re-cover, and cook on high for 30 minutes, until the chicken is tender and the vegetables are cooked through. Taste and adjust the seasoning if necessary and serve.

32

Chicken in White Wine

SERVES 4–6

2 tablespoons all-purpose flour

3 1/2-pound chicken, cut into 8 parts

4 tablespoons unsalted butter

1 tablespoon sunflower oil

4 shallots, finely chopped

12 white button mushrooms, sliced

2 tablespoons brandy

2 cups dry white wine

1 cup heavy cream

salt and pepper

cooked green vegetables,
   to serve

Method

1 Put the flour into a plastic food bag and season to taste. Add the chicken parts, in batches, hold the top securely, and shake well to coat. Transfer the chicken to a plate.

2 Heat half of the butter with the oil in a heavy skillet. Add the chicken parts, and cook over medium–high heat, turning frequently, for 10 minutes, until golden all over. Using a slotted spoon, transfer them to a plate.

3 Wipe out the skillet with paper towels, return it to medium–high heat, and melt the remaining butter. Add the shallots and mushrooms and cook, stirring continuously, for 3 minutes.

4 Return the chicken to the skillet and remove it from the heat. Warm the brandy in a small ladle, ignite, and pour it over the chicken, shaking the skillet gently until the flames have died down.

5 Return the skillet to the heat and pour in the wine. Bring to a boil over low heat, scraping up any sediment from the bottom of the skillet. Transfer to the slow cooker, cover, and cook on low for 5–6 hours, until the chicken is tender and cooked through.

6 Transfer the chicken to a serving dish and keep warm. Skim off any fat from the surface of the cooking liquid and pour the liquid into a saucepan. Stir in the cream, bring just to a boil over low heat, then pour over the chicken. Serve immediately with green vegetables.

33

Chicken & Bacon Stew

SERVES 6

4-pound chicken

4 tablespoons (1/2 stick) butter

2 tablespoons olive oil

1 1/2 pounds small white onions, peeled

1 1/2 pounds small new potatoes

6 ounces bacon, diced

2 cups dry white wine

1 bouquet garni (sprigs of parsley, bay leaf, and thyme tied together)

2 cups hot chicken stock

salt and pepper

chopped fresh flat-leaf parsley, to garnish

Method

1 Season the chicken inside and out with salt and pepper. Melt half of the butter with the oil in a large skillet. Add the chicken and cook over medium heat, turning frequently, for 8–10 minutes, until evenly browned. Remove from the skillet and put it into the slow cooker, breast side down.

2 Add the onions, potatoes, and bacon to the skillet and cook, stirring frequently, for 10 minutes, until lightly browned. Pour in the wine, season with salt and pepper, and add the bouquet garni. Bring to a boil, then transfer the mixture to the slow cooker. Pour in the hot stock. Cover and cook, turning the chicken once halfway through cooking, for 5–6 hours, until the chicken is tender and cooked through.

3 Using a slotted spoon, transfer the vegetables and bacon to a warm bowl. Carefully remove the chicken and put it on a warm serving dish. Remove and discard the bouquet garni.

4 Measure 2 1/2 cups of the cooking liquid, pour it into a saucepan, and bring to a boil. Boil until slightly reduced, then whisk in the remaining butter, a little at a time. Pour the sauce into a pitcher. Carve the chicken and transfer to individual plates with the bacon and vegetables. Garnish with parsley and serve immediately with the sauce.

Paprika Chicken

SERVES 6

2 tablespoons sunflower oil

6 chicken parts

2 onions, chopped

2 garlic cloves, finely chopped

1 fresh red chile, seeded and
finely chopped

6 tomatoes, peeled and chopped

2 teaspoons sweet paprika

1 bay leaf

1 cup hot chicken stock

salt and pepper

Method

1 Heat the oil in a large heavy skillet. Add the chicken and cook over medium heat, turning occasionally, for about 10 minutes, until evenly browned.

2 Transfer the chicken to the slow cooker and add the onions, garlic, chile, and tomatoes. Sprinkle in the paprika, add the bay leaf, and pour in the stock. Season to taste with salt and pepper. Stir well, cover, and cook on low for 6 hours, until the chicken is cooked through and tender. Remove and discard the bay leaf. Transfer to warm serving plates and serve immediately.

35

Chicken Parmigiana

SERVES 4

4 chicken parts, about
    8 ounces each

1/2 cup olive oil

3 red onions, thinly sliced

2 garlic cloves, finely chopped

1 red bell pepper, seeded and
    thinly sliced

12/3 cups sliced white button
    mushrooms

2 teaspoons chopped fresh thyme

1 tablespoon chopped fresh
    flat-leaf parsley

141/2-ounce can diced tomatoes

1/4 cup dry white vermouth

13/4 cups chicken stock

1 cup grated Parmesan cheese

salt and pepper

cooked pappardelle, to serve

Method

1 Season the chicken with salt and pepper to taste. Heat the oil in
a large, heavy saucepan. Add the chicken and cook over medium
heat for 5–6 minutes on each side, until evenly browned. Using
tongs, transfer the chicken to the slow cooker.

2 Add the onions, garlic, red bell pepper, mushrooms, thyme,
parsley, tomatoes, vermouth, and stock to the pan. Season to taste
with salt and pepper and bring to a boil, stirring occasionally.
Transfer the mixture to the slow cooker, cover, and cook on low
for 8–9 hours, until the chicken is cooked through and tender.

3 Taste and adjust the seasoning, adding salt and pepper if needed.
Transfer to warm plates and sprinkle over the Parmesan. Serve
immediately with pappardelle.

36

Nutty Chicken

SERVES 4

3 tablespoons sunflower oil

4 skinless chicken parts

2 shallots, chopped

1 teaspoon ground ginger

1 tablespoon all-purpose flour

1¾ cups beef stock

½ cup walnut pieces

grated rind of 1 lemon

2 tablespoons lemon juice

1 tablespoon black molasses

salt and pepper

pea shoots, to garnish

Method

1 Heat the oil in a large, heavy skillet. Season the chicken parts with salt and pepper and add to the skillet. Cook over medium heat, turning occasionally, for 5–8 minutes, until lightly golden all over. Transfer to the slow cooker.

2 Add the shallots to the skillet and cook, stirring occasionally, for 3–4 minutes, until softened. Sprinkle in the ginger and flour and cook, stirring continuously, for 1 minute. Gradually stir in the stock and bring to a boil, stirring continuously. Reduce the heat and simmer for 1 minute, then stir in the walnuts, lemon rind and juice, and molasses.

3 Pour the sauce over the chicken. Cover and cook on low for 6 hours, until the chicken is cooked through and tender. Taste and adjust the seasoning, adding salt and pepper if needed. Transfer the chicken to warm plates and spoon some of the sauce over each serving. Garnish with pea shoots and serve immediately.

37

Chicken Cacciatore

SERVES 4

3 tablespoons olive oil

4 skinless chicken parts

2 onions, sliced

2 garlic cloves, finely chopped

14½-ounce can diced tomatoes

1 tablespoon tomato paste

2 tablespoons chopped fresh parsley

2 teaspoons fresh thyme leaves, plus
extra sprigs to garnish

2/3 cup red wine

salt and pepper

Method

1 Heat the oil in a heavy skillet. Add the chicken and cook over medium heat, turning occasionally, for 10 minutes, until golden all over. Using a slotted spoon, transfer the chicken to the slow cooker.

2 Add the onions to the skillet and cook, stirring occasionally, for 5 minutes, until softened and just turning golden. Add the garlic, tomatoes, tomato paste, parsley, thyme leaves, and wine. Season with salt and pepper and bring to a boil.

3 Pour the tomato mixture over the chicken parts. Cover and cook on low for 5 hours, until the chicken is tender and cooked through. Taste and adjust the seasoning, adding salt and pepper if needed. Transfer to warm serving plates, garnish with thyme sprigs, and serve immediately.

38

Chipotle Chicken

SERVES 4

4–6 dried chipotle chiles

4 garlic cloves, unpeeled

1 small onion, chopped

14½-ounce can diced tomatoes

1¼ cups hot chicken stock
   or vegetable stock

4 skinless chicken breasts

salt and pepper

chopped fresh cilantro,
   to garnish

Method

1 Preheat the oven to 400°F for 15 minutes. Place the chiles in a bowl and pour in just enough hot water to cover. Set aside to soak for 30 minutes. Meanwhile, place the unpeeled garlic cloves on a baking sheet and roast in the preheated oven for about 10 minutes, until soft. Remove from the oven and set aside to cool.

2 Drain the chiles, reserving ½ cup of the soaking water. Seed the chiles, if you like, and chop coarsely. Place the chiles and reserved soaking water in a blender or food processor and process to a puree. Peel and mash the garlic in a bowl.

3 Place the chili puree, garlic, onion, and tomatoes in the slow cooker and stir in the stock. Season the chicken with salt and pepper and place in the slow cooker. Cover and cook on low for about 5 hours, until the chicken is tender and cooked through.

4 Lift the chicken out of the slow cooker with a slotted spoon, cover, and keep warm. Pour the cooking liquid into a saucepan and bring to a boil on the stove. Boil for 5–10 minutes, until reduced. Transfer the chicken to warm serving plates and pour the sauce over the chicken. Serve immediately garnished with cilantro.

39

Slow Roasted Chicken

SERVES 4–6

3¼-pound oven-ready chicken
½ lemon
1 tablespoon olive oil
½ teaspoon dried thyme
½ teaspoon paprika
salt and pepper

Method

1 Wipe the chicken with paper towels and tuck the lemon half inside the body cavity. Brush the oil over the chicken skin and sprinkle with thyme, paprika, and salt and pepper, rubbing in with your fingers to cover all the skin.

2 Place the chicken in the slow cooker, cover, and cook on high for 3 hours. Reduce the heat to low and cook for an additional 4 hours, until the chicken is tender.

3 Carefully remove the chicken and place on a warm serving plate, then skim any fat from the juices. Adjust the seasoning to taste and serve.

40

Chicken Quesadillas

SERVES 4

4 skinless chicken breasts

1/2 teaspoon crushed red pepper

2 garlic cloves, crushed

2 tablespoons finely chopped parsley

2 tablespoons olive oil

2 1/2 cups cherry tomatoes

4 large whole-wheat tortillas

8 ounces mozzarella cheese

salt and pepper

Method

1 Place the chicken in a bowl with the crushed red pepper, garlic, parsley, and 1 tablespoon of the olive oil, and turn to coat evenly. Cover and let stand in the refrigerator to marinate for at least 1 hour, or overnight.

2 Put the tomatoes into the slow cooker and arrange the chicken breasts on top. Season with salt and pepper. Cover and cook on high for 2 hours, until tender.

3 Remove the chicken and shred the meat using two forks. Place on one side of each tortilla and top with the tomatoes. Chop or tear the mozzarella and arrange on top. Moisten the edges of the tortillas and fold over to enclose the filling.

4 Brush a flat griddle pan or large skillet with the remaining oil and place over medium heat. Add the quesadillas to the pan and cook until golden, turning once. Cut into wedges and serve. Any spare juices can be spooned over.

Barbecue Chicken

SERVES 4

8 skinless chicken drumsticks
  or thighs

3 tablespoons tomato paste

2 tablespoons honey

1 tablespoon Worcestershire sauce

juice of 1/2 lemon

1/2 teaspoon crushed red pepper

1 garlic clove, crushed

salt and pepper

Method

1 Using a sharp knife, cut slashes into the thickest parts of the chicken flesh.

2 Mix together the tomato paste, honey, Worcestershire sauce, lemon juice, crushed red pepper, and garlic and season with salt and pepper. Add the chicken and toss well to coat evenly.

3 Arrange the chicken in the slow cooker, cover, and cook on high for 3 hours.

4 Remove the chicken with a slotted spoon and transfer to a warm serving dish. Spoon the juices over the chicken, skimming off any fat. Serve immediately.

Sweet & Sour Chicken Wings

SERVES 4–6

2¼ pounds chicken wings,
  tips removed

2 celery stalks, chopped

3 cups hot chicken stock

2 tablespoons cornstarch

3 tablespoons white wine vinegar or
  rice vinegar

3 tablespoons dark soy sauce

⅓ cup sweet chili sauce

¼ cup firmly packed light
  brown sugar

two 8-ounce cans pineapple chunks
  in juice, drained

8-ounce can sliced bamboo shoots,
  drained and rinsed

½ green bell pepper, seeded and
  thinly sliced

½ red bell pepper, seeded and
  thinly sliced

salt

steamed bok choy, to serve

Method

1 Put the chicken wings and celery in the slow cooker and season well with salt. Pour in the stock, cover, and cook on low for 5 hours.

2 Drain the chicken wings, reserving 1½ cups of the stock, and keep warm. Pour the reserved stock into a saucepan and stir in the cornstarch. Add the vinegar, soy sauce, and chili sauce. Place over medium heat and stir in the sugar. Cook, stirring continuously, for 5 minutes, or until the sugar has dissolved completely and the sauce is thickened, smooth, and clear.

3 Reduce the heat, stir in the pineapple, bamboo shoots, and bell peppers, and simmer gently for 2–3 minutes. Stir in the chicken wings until they are thoroughly coated, then transfer to warm serving bowls. Serve immediately with bok choy.

43

Easy Chinese Chicken

SERVES 4

2 teaspoons grated fresh ginger

4 garlic cloves, finely chopped

2 star anise or 1 teaspoon five-spice
    powder

2/3 cup Chinese rice wine or medium-
    dry sherry

2 tablespoons dark soy sauce

1 teaspoon sesame oil

1/3 cup water

4 skinless chicken thighs
    or drumsticks

shredded scallions, to garnish

cooked rice, to serve

Method

1 Mix together the ginger, garlic, star anise, rice wine, soy sauce, sesame oil, and water in a bowl. Place the chicken in a saucepan, add the spice mixture, and bring to a boil.

2 Transfer to the slow cooker, cover, and cook on low for 4 hours, or until the chicken is tender and cooked through.

3 Remove and discard the star anise. Transfer the chicken to warm serving plates, garnish with shredded scallions, and serve immediately with rice.

Parmesan Chicken

SERVES 4

1 egg, beaten

4 skinless, boneless chicken breasts

1 cup fine dry bread crumbs

2 tablespoons olive oil

*1½ cups store-bought,
tomato-based pasta sauce*

*4 slices American cheese
or cheddar cheese*

*1¼ cups finely grated Parmesan
cheese*

salt and pepper

cooked rice, to serve

Method

1 Season the egg with salt and pepper. Dip each chicken breast in the egg, turning to coat evenly, then dip into the bread crumbs, lightly pressing down to cover evenly.

2 Heat the oil in a skillet over high heat, add the chicken breasts, and cook quickly for 3–4 minutes, until golden brown, turning once.

3 Pour the pasta sauce into the slow cooker and place the chicken breasts on top. Cover and cook on low for 4 hours.

4 Place a slice of American cheese on top of each chicken breast and sprinkle with Parmesan cheese. Cover and cook on high for an additional 20 minutes. Transfer to a warm serving dish and serve immediately with rice.

45

Chicken Braised with Cabbage

SERVES 4

2 tablespoons sunflower oil

4 skinless chicken thighs
   or drumsticks

1 onion, chopped

5 cups shredded red cabbage

2 apples, such as Idared or Pippin,
   peeled and chopped

12 canned or cooked chestnuts,
   halved (optional)

1/2 teaspoon juniper berries or
   2 teaspoons gin

1/2 cup red wine

salt and pepper

chopped fresh flat-leaf parsley,
   to garnish

Method

1 Heat the oil in a large, heavy saucepan. Add the chicken and cook, turning frequently, for 5 minutes, until golden on all sides. Using a slotted spoon, transfer to a plate lined with paper towels.
2 Add the onion to the saucepan and cook over medium heat, stirring occasionally, until softened. Stir in the cabbage and apples and cook, stirring occasionally, for 5 minutes. Add the chestnuts, if using, juniper berries, and wine and season to taste with salt and pepper. Bring to a boil.
3 Spoon half of the cabbage mixture into the slow cooker, add the chicken parts, then top with the remaining cabbage mixture. Cover and cook on low for 5 hours, until the chicken is tender and cooked through. Transfer to warm serving bowls, garnish with parsley, and serve immediately.

46

Turkey Meatloaf

SERVES 4

oil for greasing

1 1/4 pounds ground turkey

1 onion, finely chopped

2/3 cup rolled oats

2 tablespoons chopped fresh sage

2 tablespoons Worcestershire sauce

1 egg, beaten

salt and pepper

Method

1 Grease and line a 9-inch loaf pan or another baking pan that fits into your slow cooker.

2 Mix together the ground turkey, onion, oats, sage, Worcestershire sauce, egg, salt and pepper.

3 Spoon the mixture into the prepared pan and smooth the top level with a spatula.

4 Place the loaf in the slow cooker and place a piece of parchment paper on top. Cover and cook on low for 4 hours, until firm and the juices are clear, not pink.

5 Invert the loaf and serve sliced.

47

Turkey & Rice Casserole

SERVES 4

1 tablespoon olive oil

1 pound turkey breast, diced

1 onion, diced

2 carrots, diced

2 celery stalks, sliced

3½ cups sliced white button
    mushrooms

1 cup long-grain rice

2 cups hot chicken stock

salt and pepper

Method

1 Heat the oil in a heavy skillet, add the turkey, and cook over high heat for 3–4 minutes, until lightly browned.

2 Combine the onion, carrots, celery, mushrooms, and rice in the slow cooker. Arrange the turkey on top, season well with salt and pepper, and pour the stock over. Cover and cook on high for 2 hours.

3 Stir lightly with a fork to mix, adjust the seasoning to taste and serve immediately.

48

Turkey Hash

SERVES 4

1 tablespoon olive oil

1 pound ground turkey

1 large red onion, diced

4¼ cups diced butternut squash

2 celery stalks, sliced

4 potatoes, such as russets, white rounders, or Yukon gold, peeled and diced

3 tablespoons Worcestershire sauce

2 bay leaves

salt and pepper

Method

1 Heat the oil in a skillet, add the turkey, and cook over high heat, stirring, until broken up and lightly browned.

2 Place all the vegetables in the slow cooker, then add the turkey and pan juices. Add the Worcestershire sauce and bay leaves and season with salt and pepper. Cover and cook on low for 7 hours. Remove and discard the bay leaves. Transfer to warm serving bowls and serve immediately.

49

Turkey Pasta Casserole

SERVES 4

9 ounces dried macaroni
¾ cup tomato juice
1 pound ground turkey
1 small onion, finely chopped
1 cup fresh white bread crumbs
⅓ cup pesto sauce
4 ounces mozzarella cheese
salt and pepper
fresh basil leaves, to garnish

Method

1 Bring a large saucepan of lightly salted water to a boil, add the pasta, return to a boil, and cook for 5–6 minutes, or half the amount of time given in the package directions. Drain well, place in the slow cooker, and stir in the tomato juice.

2 Mix the turkey, onion, and bread crumbs together. Season well with salt and pepper. Divide the mixture into about 20 small balls, rolling them with your hands.

3 Arrange the meatballs over the pasta in a single layer and spoon a little of the pesto sauce on top of each. Cover and cook on high for 2 hours.

4 Tear the mozzarella cheese into small pieces and scatter over the meatballs. Cover and cook on high for an additional 20 minutes. Serve immediately, garnished with fresh basil.

3

FISH & SEAFOOD

50

New England Clam Chowder

SERVES 4

2 tablespoons salted butter

1 onion, finely chopped

2 potatoes, peeled and
    cut into cubes

1 large carrot, diced

1¾ cups fish stock or water

10-ounce can clams, drained

1 cup heavy cream

salt and pepper

chopped fresh parsley, to garnish

fresh crusty bread, to serve

Method

1 Melt the butter in a skillet, add the onion, and sauté over medium heat for 4–5 minutes, stirring, until golden.

2 Transfer the onion to the slow cooker with the potatoes, carrot, stock, and salt and pepper. Cover and cook on high for 3 hours.

3 Add the clams and the cream to the slow cooker and stir to mix evenly. Cover and cook for an additional 1 hour.

4 Adjust the seasoning to taste. Transfer to warm serving bowls, sprinkle with parsley, and serve immediately with crusty bread.

Salmon Chowder

SERVES 4

1 tablespoon salted butter

1 tablespoon sunflower oil

1 onion, finely chopped

1 leek, finely chopped

*1 fennel bulb, finely chopped,
feathery tops reserved*

2 cups diced potatoes

3 cups fish stock

*1-pound salmon fillet, skinned
and cut into cubes*

1¼ cups milk

2/3 cup light cream

2 tablespoons chopped fresh dill

salt and pepper

Method

1 Melt the butter with the oil in a saucepan. Add the onion, leek, and fennel and cook over low heat, stirring occasionally, for 5 minutes. Add the potatoes and cook, stirring occasionally, for an additional 4 minutes, then pour in the stock and season to taste with salt and pepper. Bring to a boil, then transfer to the slow cooker. Cover and cook on low for 3 hours, until the potatoes are tender.

2 Meanwhile, chop the fennel tops and set aside. Add the salmon to the slow cooker, pour in the milk, and stir gently. Re-cover and cook on low for 30 minutes, until the fish flakes easily.

3 Gently stir in the cream, dill, and the reserved fennel tops, re-cover, and cook for an additional 10–15 minutes, until heated through. Taste and adjust the seasoning, adding salt and pepper if needed. Serve immediately.

52

Salmon with Dill & Lime

SERVES 4

3 tablespoons salted butter, melted

1 onion, thinly sliced

4 potatoes, peeled and thinly sliced

1/2 cup hot fish stock or water

4 pieces skinless salmon fillet,
   about 5 ounces each

juice of 1 lime

2 tablespoons chopped fresh dill

salt and pepper

lime wedges, to serve

Method

1 Brush the bottom of the slow cooker with 1 tablespoon of the butter. Layer the onion and potatoes in the dish, sprinkling with salt and pepper between the layers. Add the stock and drizzle with 1 tablespoon of the butter. Cover and cook on low for 3 hours.

2 Arrange the salmon over the vegetables in a single layer. Drizzle the lime juice over, sprinkle with dill and salt and pepper, and pour the remaining butter on top. Cover and cook on low for an additional 1 hour, until the fish flakes easily.

3 Serve the salmon and vegetables on warm plates with the juices spooned over and lime wedges on the side.

53

Salmon Florentine

SERVES 4

2/3 cup fish stock

1 cup dry white wine

2 lemons

1 onion, thinly sliced

4 salmon fillets, about
6 ounces each

1 bouquet garni (sprigs of parsley,
bay leaf, and thyme tied together)

3 pounds spinach, trimmed

freshly grated nutmeg, to taste

3/4 cup (1 1/2 sticks) unsalted butter,
plus extra for greasing

salt and pepper

Method

1 Lightly grease the slow cooker pot with butter. Pour the stock and wine into a saucepan and bring to a boil. Meanwhile, thinly slice one of the lemons. Put half of the lemon slices and all the onion slices over the bottom of the slow cooker pot and top with the salmon fillets. Season to taste with salt and pepper, add the bouquet garni, and cover the fish with the remaining lemon slices. Pour the hot stock mixture over the fish, cover, and cook on low for 1 1/2 hours, until the fish flakes easily.

2 Meanwhile, finely grate the rind and squeeze the juice from the remaining lemon. When the fish is nearly ready, cook the spinach, in just the water clinging to the leaves after washing, for 3–5 minutes, until wilted. Drain well, squeezing out as much water as possible. Chop finely, arrange on a warm serving dish, and season to taste with salt, pepper, and nutmeg.

3 Carefully lift the fish out of the slow cooker with a spatula and discard the lemon slices, onion slices, and bouquet garni. Put the salmon fillets on the bed of spinach and keep warm.

4 Melt the butter in a saucepan over low heat. Stir in the lemon rind and half of the juice. Taste and adjust the seasoning, adding more lemon juice, salt, and pepper if needed. Pour the lemon-butter sauce over the fish and serve immediately.

Sea Bream in Lemon Sauce

SERVES 4

8 sea bream or red snapper fillets

4 tablespoons (1/2 stick) unsalted butter

3 tablespoons all-purpose flour

3 1/2 cups warm milk

1/4 cup lemon juice

3 cups sliced white button mushrooms

1 bouquet garni (sprigs of parsley, bay leaf, and thyme tied together)

salt and pepper

lemon wedges and pan-grilled asparagus, to serve

Method

1 Put the fish fillets into the slow cooker and set aside.

2 Melt the butter in a saucepan over low heat. Add the flour and cook, stirring continuously, for 1 minute. Gradually stir in the milk, a little at a time, and bring to a boil, stirring continuously. Stir in the lemon juice and mushrooms, add the bouquet garni, and season to taste with salt and pepper. Reduce the heat and simmer for 5 minutes. Pour the sauce over the fish fillets, cover, and cook on low for 1 1/2 hours.

3 Carefully lift out the fish fillets and transfer to warm serving plates. Serve immediately with lemon wedges and asparagus.

55

Moroccan Sea Bass

SERVES 2

2 tablespoons olive oil

2 onions, chopped

2 garlic cloves, finely chopped

2 carrots, finely chopped

1 fennel bulb, finely chopped

1/2 teaspoon ground cumin

1/2 teaspoon ground cloves

1 teaspoon ground coriander

pinch of saffron threads

1 1/4 cups fish stock

1 preserved or fresh lemon

2-pound sea bass, cleaned

salt and pepper

Method

1 Heat the oil in a large heavy saucepan. Add the onions, garlic, carrots, and fennel and cook over medium heat, stirring occasionally, for 5 minutes. Stir in all the spices and cook, stirring, for an additional 2 minutes. Pour in the stock, season to taste with salt and pepper, and bring to a boil.

2 Transfer the mixture to the slow cooker. Cover and cook on low for 6 hours, or until the vegetables are tender.

3 Rinse the preserved lemon. Discard the fish head, if you like. Slice the lemon and place the slices in the fish cavity, then place the fish in the slow cooker on top of the vegetables. Re-cover and cook on high for 30–45 minutes, until the flesh flakes easily.

4 Carefully transfer the fish to a serving plate and spoon the vegetables around it, using a slotted spoon. Cover and keep warm. Transfer the cooking liquid to a saucepan and boil for a few minutes until reduced. Spoon the sauce over the fish and serve immediately.

56

Tilapia with Oranges

SERVES 4

4 tilapia, about
    12 ounces each, cleaned

1 orange, halved and thinly sliced

2 garlic cloves, thinly sliced

6 fresh thyme sprigs

1 tablespoon olive oil

1 fennel bulb, thinly sliced

2 cups orange juice

1 bay leaf

1 teaspoon dill seeds

salt and pepper

salad greens, to serve

Method

1 Season the fish inside and outside with salt and pepper. Make 3–4 diagonal slashes on each side. Divide the orange slices among the cavities and add 2–3 garlic slices and a thyme sprig to each. Put the remaining garlic and thyme in the slashes.

2 Heat the oil in a large skillet. Add the fennel and cook over medium heat, stirring frequently, for 3–5 minutes, until just softened. Add the orange juice and bay leaf and bring to a boil, then reduce the heat and simmer for an additional 5 minutes.

3 Transfer the fennel mixture to the slow cooker. Put the fish on top and sprinkle with the dill seeds. Cover and cook on high for 1 1/4–1 1/2 hours, until the flesh flakes easily.

4 Carefully transfer the fish to warm individual plates. Remove and discard the bay leaf. Spoon the fennel and some of the cooking juices over the fish and serve immediately with salad greens.

Tilapia Casserole

SERVES 4

1 tablespoon olive oil

1 red onion, sliced

1 yellow bell pepper, seeded
   and sliced

4 tilapia fillets, about 5 ounces each

2 tomatoes, thinly sliced

8 pitted black ripe olives, halved

1 garlic clove, thinly sliced

2 teaspoons balsamic vinegar

juice of 1 orange

salt and pepper

Method

1 Heat the oil in a skillet, add the onion and yellow bell pepper, and fry over high heat for 3–4 minutes, stirring, until lightly browned. Transfer to the slow cooker, cover, and cook on high for 1 hour.

2 Arrange the fish fillets over the vegetables and season with salt and pepper. Arrange a layer of tomatoes and olives over the top and sprinkle with the garlic, vinegar, and salt and pepper. Pour over the orange juice, cover, and cook on high for an additional 1 hour. Transfer to warm serving plates and serve immediately.

58

Sole & Shrimp with Cream Sauc

SERVES 4

8 potatoes (about 2 pounds),
   cut into chunks

1 1/2 pounds sole fillets

2 tablespoons salted butter,
   plus extra for greasing

2 egg yolks

1 1/2 cups shredded cheddar cheese
   or American cheese

1 tablespoon chopped fresh
   flat-leaf parsley, plus extra
   sprigs to garnish

1 1/4 pounds cooked, peeled shrimp

salt and pepper

Method

1 Put the potatoes into a saucepan, pour in water to cover, add a pinch of salt, and bring to a boil. Reduce the heat, cover, and cook for 20–25 minutes, until soft but not falling apart.

2 Meanwhile, grease a 1 1/4-quart casserole dish with butter, then line it with the fish fillets, skin side inward and with the tail ends overlapping the rim. Cut out a double circle of wax paper that is 2 inches wider than the rim of the dish. Grease one side with butter.

3 Drain the potatoes in a colander. Return to the saucepan, add the butter, and reheat gently until it has melted. Remove from the heat and mash well, then stir in the egg yolks, cheese, and parsley. Season lightly with salt and pepper.

4 Make alternating layers of the mashed potato mixture and shrimp in the casserole dish, then fold over the overlapping fish fillets. Cover the dish with the wax paper circles and tie in place with string.

5 Stand the dish on a trivet in the slow cooker and pour in enough boiling water to come about halfway up the side. Cover and cook on low for 2 1/2 hours.

6 Carefully remove the casserole dish from the slow cooker and discard the wax paper. Invert onto a warm serving dish. Garnish with parsley sprigs and serve immediately.

59

Tuna Noodle Casserole

SERVES 4

8 ounces dried egg tagliatelle

three 5-ounce cans tuna steak
   in oil, drained

1 bunch scallions, sliced

1¼ cups frozen peas

2 teaspoons hot chili sauce

2½ cups hot chicken stock

1 cup shredded cheddar cheese
   or American cheese

salt and pepper

Method

1 Bring a large saucepan of lightly salted water to a boil. Add the pasta, return to a boil, and cook for 2 minutes, until the pasta ribbons are loose. Drain.

2 Break up the tuna into bite-size chunks and place in the slow cooker with the pasta, scallions, and peas. Season to taste with salt and pepper.

3 Add the chili sauce to the stock and pour over the ingredients in the slow cooker. Sprinkle the shredded cheese over the top. Cover and cook on low for 2 hours. Serve immediately on warm plates.

60

French-style Fish Stew

SERVES 4–6

large pinch of saffron threads

1 prepared squid

2 pounds mixed white fish, such as
   sea bass or monkfish, filleted and
   cut into large chunks

24 large shrimp, peeled and
   deveined, heads and shells
   reserved

2 tablespoons olive oil

1 large onion, finely chopped

1 fennel bulb, thinly sliced,
   feathery tops reserved

2 large garlic cloves, crushed

1/4 cup Pernod

41/4 cups fish stock

141/2-ounce can diced tomatoes,
   drained

1 tablespoon tomato paste

1 bay leaf

pinch of sugar

salt and pepper

Method

1 Toast the saffron threads in a dry skillet over high heat for 1 minute. Set side. Cut off and reserve the tentacles from the squid and slice the body into 1/4-inch rings. Place the seafood and fish in a bowl, cover, and chill in the refrigerator until required. Tie the heads and shells of the shrimp in a piece of cheesecloth.

2 Heat the oil in a skillet. Add the onion and fennel and cook over low heat, for 5 minutes. Add the garlic and cook for 2 minutes. Remove the skillet from the heat. Heat the Pernod in a saucepan, ignite, and pour it over the onion and fennel, gently shaking the skillet until the flames die down.

3 Return the skillet to the heat, stir in the toasted saffron, stock, tomatoes, tomato paste, bay leaf and sugar, and season with salt and pepper. Bring to a boil, then transfer to the slow cooker, add the bag of shrimp shells, cover, and cook on low for 6 hours.

4 Remove and discard the bag of shrimp shells and the bay leaf. Add the fish and seafood to the slow cooker, cover, and cook on high for 30 minutes, until the fish flakes easily. Serve garnished with the reserved fennel tops.

Shellfish Stew

SERVES 8

1 tablespoon olive oil

4 ounces bacon, diced

2 tablespoons salted butter

2 shallots, chopped

2 leeks, sliced

2 celery stalks, chopped

2 potatoes, diced

6 tomatoes (about 1 1/2 pounds),
   peeled, seeded, and chopped

3 tablespoons chopped fresh parsley

3 tablespoons snipped fresh chives,
   plus extra to garnish

1 bay leaf

1 fresh thyme sprig

6 cups fish stock

24 fresh mussels

24 fresh clams

1 pound sea bream fillets

24 jumbo shrimp

salt and pepper

Method

1 Heat the oil in a heavy skillet. Add the bacon and cook, stirring frequently, for 5–8 minutes, until crisp. Using a slotted spoon, transfer to the slow cooker. Add the butter to the skillet and when it has melted, add the shallots, leeks, celery, and potatoes. Cook over low heat, stirring occasionally, for 5 minutes, until softened. Stir in the tomatoes, parsley, chives, bay leaf, and thyme, pour in the stock, and bring to a boil, stirring continuously. Pour the mixture into the slow cooker, cover, and cook on low for 7 hours.

2 Meanwhile, scrub the mussels and clams under cold running water and pull off the "beards" from the mussels. Discard any with broken shells or that do not shut immediately when sharply tapped. Cut the fish fillets into bite-size chunks. Peel and devein the shrimp.

3 Remove the bay leaf and thyme sprig from the stew and discard. Season with salt and pepper and add all the fish and seafood. Re-cover and cook on high for 30 minutes. Discard any shellfish that remain closed. Serve garnished with extra chives.

Seafood Gumbo

SERVES 6

2 tablespoons sunflower oil

15 okra pods, trimmed and
cut into 1-inch pieces

2 onions, finely chopped

4 celery stalks, finely chopped

1 garlic clove, finely chopped

2 tablespoons all-purpose flour

1/2 teaspoon sugar

1 teaspoon ground cumin

3 cups fish stock

1 red bell pepper, seeded
and chopped

1 green bell pepper, seeded
and chopped

2 large tomatoes, chopped

1/4 cup chopped fresh parsley

1 tablespoon chopped fresh cilantro

Tabasco sauce

12 ounces large, fresh shrimp,
peeled and deveined

12 ounces cod or haddock fillets,
skinned and cut into 1-inch
chunks

12 ounces monkfish fillet, cut into
1-inch chunks

salt and pepper

Method

1 Heat half of the oil in a heavy skillet. Add the okra and cook over low heat, stirring frequently, for 5 minutes, until browned. Using a slotted spoon, transfer the okra to the slow cooker.

2 Add the remaining oil to the skillet. Add the onions and celery and cook over low heat, stirring occasionally, for 5 minutes, until softened. Add the garlic and cook, stirring frequently, for 1 minute, then sprinkle in the flour, sugar, and cumin and season with salt and pepper. Cook, stirring continuously, for 2 minutes, then remove the skillet from the heat.

3 Gradually stir in the stock, then return the skillet to the heat and bring to a boil, stirring continuously. Pour the mixture over the okra and stir in the bell peppers and tomatoes. Cover and cook on low for 5–6 hours.

4 Stir in the parsley, cilantro, and Tabasco to taste, then add the shrimp, cod, and monkfish. Cover and cook on high for 30 minutes, until the fish is cooked and the shrimp have changed color. Taste and adjust the seasoning, if necessary, and serve.

Jambalaya

SERVES 4

1/2 teaspoon cayenne pepper

2 teaspoons chopped fresh thyme

12 ounces skinless, boneless chicken
    breasts, diced

2 tablespoons corn oil

2 onions, chopped

2 garlic cloves, finely chopped

2 green bell peppers, seeded
    and chopped

2 celery stalks, chopped

4 ounces smoked ham, chopped

6 ounces chorizo sausage, sliced

141/2-ounce can diced tomatoes

2 tablespoons tomato paste

1 cup chicken stock

1 pound shrimp, peeled and
    deveined

2 cups freshly cooked rice

salt and pepper

snipped fresh chives, to garnish

Method

1 Mix together the cayenne pepper, 1/2 teaspoon of pepper, 1 teaspoon of salt, and the thyme in a bowl. Add the chicken and toss to coat.

2 Heat the oil in a large, heavy saucepan. Add the onions, garlic, green bell peppers, and celery and cook over low heat, stirring occasionally, for 5 minutes. Add the chicken and cook over medium heat, stirring frequently, for an additional 5 minutes, until golden all over. Stir in the ham, chorizo, tomatoes, tomato paste, and stock and bring to a boil.

3 Transfer the mixture to the slow cooker. Cover and cook on low for 6 hours. Add the shrimp and rice, re-cover, and cook on high for 30 minutes.

4 Taste and adjust the seasoning, adding salt and pepper if necessary. Transfer to warm plates, garnish with chives, and serve immediately.

Bouillabaisse

SERVES 6

5 pounds mixed white fish,
    such as red snapper, sea bream,
    sea bass, monkfish, and whiting,
    filleted and bones and heads
    reserved, if possible

1 pound shrimp

grated rind of 1 orange

pinch of saffron threads

4 garlic cloves, finely chopped

1 cup olive oil

2 onions, finely chopped

1 leek, thinly sliced

4 potatoes, thinly sliced

2 large tomatoes, peeled
    and chopped

1 bunch fresh flat-leaf parsley,
    chopped

1 fresh fennel sprig

1 fresh thyme sprig

1 bay leaf

2 cloves

6 black peppercorns

1 strip thinly pared orange rind

sea salt

lightly toasted crusty bread,
    to serve

Method

1 Cut the fish fillets into bite-size pieces. Peel and devein the shrimp, reserving the heads and shells. Rinse the fish bones, if using, and cut away the gills from the fish heads. Place the chunks of fish and the shrimp in a large bowl. Sprinkle with the grated orange rind, saffron, half of the garlic, and 2 tablespoons of the oil. Cover and set aside in the refrigerator.

2 Put the remaining garlic, the onions, leek, potatoes, tomatoes, parsley, fennel, thyme, bay leaf, cloves, peppercorns, and strip of orange rind into the slow cooker. Add the fish heads and bones, if using, and the shrimp shells and heads. Pour in the remaining oil and enough boiling water to cover the ingredients by 1 inch. Season to taste with sea salt. Cover and cook on low for 8 hours.

3 Strain the stock and return the liquid to the slow cooker. Discard the flavorings, fish, and shrimp trimmings but reserve the vegetables and return them to the slow cooker, if you like. Add the fish-and-shrimp mixture, re-cover, and cook on high for 30 minutes, until the fish is cooked through and flakes easily.

4 Ladle into warm bowls and serve immediately with toasted crusty bread.

65

Green Chili Seafood Stew

SERVES 4

2 tablespoons olive oil

1 large onion, chopped

4 garlic cloves, finely chopped

1 yellow bell pepper, seeded and chopped

1 red bell pepper, seeded and chopped

1 orange bell pepper, seeded and chopped

4 tomatoes, peeled and chopped

2 large mild green chiles, such as poblano, chopped

finely grated rind and juice of 1 lime

2 tablespoons chopped fresh cilantro, plus extra leaves to garnish

1 bay leaf

2 cups fish stock, vegetable stock, or chicken stock

1 pound red snapper fillets

1 pound shrimp

8 ounces prepared squid

salt and pepper

Method

1 Heat the oil in a saucepan. Add the onion and garlic and cook over low heat, stirring occasionally, for 5 minutes, until softened. Add the bell peppers, tomatoes, and chiles and cook, stirring frequently, for 5 minutes. Stir in the lime rind and juice, add the chopped cilantro and bay leaf, and pour in the stock. Bring to a boil, stirring occasionally.

2 Transfer the mixture to the slow cooker, cover, and cook on low for 7 1/2 hours. Meanwhile, skin the fish fillets, if necessary, and cut the flesh into chunks. Peel and devein the shrimp. Cut the squid bodies into rings, and halve the tentacles or leave them whole.

3 Add the seafood to the stew, season to taste with salt and pepper, re-cover, and cook on high for 30 minutes, or until tender and cooked through. Remove and discard the bay leaf. Transfer to warm serving bowls, garnish with cilantro leaves, and serve immediately.

Seafood in Saffron Sauce

SERVES 4

2 tablespoons olive oil

1 onion, sliced

2 celery stalks, sliced

pinch of saffron threads

1 tablespoon chopped fresh thyme

2 garlic cloves, finely chopped

28-ounce can diced tomatoes,
   drained

3/4 cup dry white wine

9 cups fish stock

8 ounces fresh clams

8 ounces fresh mussels

12 ounces red snapper fillets

1 pound monkfish fillet

8 ounces squid rings, thawed
   if frozen

2 tablespoons shredded,
   fresh basil leaves

salt and pepper

Method

1 Heat the oil in a heavy skillet. Add the onion, celery, saffron, thyme, and a pinch of salt and cook over low heat, stirring occasionally, for 5 minutes until softened. Add the garlic and cook, stirring continuously, for 2 minutes.

2 Add the tomatoes, wine, and stock, season with salt and pepper, and bring to a boil, stirring continuously. Transfer the mixture to the slow cooker, cover, and cook on low for 5 hours.

3 Meanwhile, scrub the shellfish under cold running water and pull the "beards" off the mussels. Discard any with broken shells or that do not shut immediately when sharply tapped. Cut the red snapper and monkfish fillets into bite-size chunks.

4 Add the pieces of fish, the shellfish, and squid rings to the slow cooker, re-cover, and cook on high for 30 minutes, until the clams and mussels have opened and the fish is cooked through. Discard any shellfish that remain closed. Stir in the basil and serve.

Tagliatelle with Shrimp

SERVES 4

3 tomatoes, peeled
and chopped

1/2 cup tomato paste

1 garlic clove, finely chopped

2 tablespoons chopped fresh parsley

1 pound cooked, peeled shrimp

6 fresh basil leaves, torn,
plus extra to garnish

14 ounces dried tagliatelle

salt and pepper

Method

1 Put the tomatoes, tomato paste, garlic, and parsley in the slow cooker and season with salt and pepper. Cover and cook on low for 7 hours.

2 Add the shrimp and basil. Re-cover and cook on high for 15 minutes.

3 Meanwhile, bring a large saucepan of lightly salted water to a boil. Add the pasta, bring back to a boil, and cook for 10–12 minutes, until tender but still firm to the bite.

4 Drain the pasta and transfer to a warm serving bowl. Add the shrimp sauce and toss lightly with two large forks. Garnish with the basil leaves and serve immediately.

4

VEGETARIAN

Tomato & Lentil Soup

SERVES 4

2 tablespoons sunflower oil

1 onion, chopped

1 garlic clove, finely chopped

2 celery stalks, chopped

2 carrots, chopped

1 teaspoon ground cumin

1 teaspoon ground coriander

1 cup of canned red or yellow lentils, rinsed and drained

1 tablespoon tomato paste

5 cups vegetable stock

14½-ounce can diced tomatoes

1 bay leaf

salt and pepper

crème fraîche or Greek-style yogurt, to serve

toasted crusty bread, to serve

Method

1 Heat the oil in a saucepan. Add the onion and garlic and cook over low heat, stirring occasionally, for 5 minutes, until softened. Stir in the celery and carrots and cook, stirring occasionally, for an additional 4 minutes. Stir in the ground cumin and coriander and cook, stirring, for 1 minute, then add the lentils.

2 Mix the tomato paste with a little of the stock in a small bowl and add to the pan with the remaining stock, the tomatoes, and bay leaf. Bring to a boil, then transfer to the slow cooker. Stir well, cover, and cook on low for 3½–4 hours.

3 Remove and discard the bay leaf. Transfer the soup to a food processor or blender and process until smooth. Season to taste with salt and pepper. Ladle into warm soup bowls, top each with a swirl of crème fraîche, and serve immediately with toasted crusty bread.

69

Carrot & Cilantro Soup

SERVES 6

1 tablespoon butter

1 1/2 tablespoons sunflower oil

1 Bermuda onion, finely chopped

8 carrots, diced

1/2-inch piece fresh ginger

2 teaspoons ground coriander

1 teaspoon all-purpose flour

5 cups vegetable stock

2/3 cup sour cream

salt and pepper

2 tablespoons chopped fresh
    cilantro, to garnish

croutons, to serve

Method

1 Melt the butter with the oil in a saucepan. Add the onion, carrots, and ginger, cover, and cook over low heat, stirring occasionally, for 8 minutes, until softened and just beginning to color.

2 Sprinkle over the ground coriander and flour and cook, stirring thoroughly, for 1 minute. Gradually stir in the stock, a little at a time, and bring to a boil, stirring thoroughly. Season to taste with salt and pepper.

3 Transfer the mixture to the slow cooker, cover, and cook on low for 4–5 hours. Ladle the soup into a food processor or blender, in batches if necessary, and process until smooth. Return the soup to the slow cooker and stir in the sour cream. Cover and cook on low for an additional 15–20 minutes, until heated through.

4 Ladle the soup into warm soup bowls, garnish with the chopped cilantro and sprinkle with croutons. Serve immediately.

70

Greek Bean & Vegetable Soup

SERVES 4–6

2½ cups dried cannellini beans,
    soaked in cold water overnight
    or for at least 5 hours, drained,
    and rinsed

2 onions, finely chopped

2 garlic cloves, finely chopped

2 potatoes, chopped

2 carrots, chopped

2 tomatoes, peeled and chopped

2 celery stalks, chopped

¼ cup extra virgin olive oil

1 bay leaf

salt and pepper

12 ripe black olives, to garnish

2 tablespoons snipped fresh chives,
    to garnish

Method

1 Put the beans in a saucepan, cover with fresh water, and bring to a boil. Boil rapidly for at least 10 minutes, then drain and rinse again. Place the beans in the slow cooker and add the onions, garlic, potatoes, carrots, tomatoes, celery, olive oil, and bay leaf.

2 Pour in 9 cups of boiling water, making sure that all the ingredients are fully submerged. Cover and cook on low for 12 hours, until the beans are tender.

3 Remove and discard the bay leaf. Season the soup to taste with salt and pepper and garnish with the olives and chives. Transfer to warm soup bowls and serve.

Louisiana Zucchini

SERVES 6

7 zucchini (about 2¼ pounds),
   thickly sliced

1 onion, finely chopped

2 garlic cloves, finely chopped

2 red bell peppers, seeded
   and chopped

⅓ cup hot vegetable stock

4 tomatoes, peeled and chopped

2 tablespoons butter, diced

salt and cayenne pepper

crusty bread, to serve

Method

1 Place the zucchini, onion, garlic, and red bell peppers in the slow cooker and season to taste with salt and cayenne pepper. Pour in the stock and mix well.

2 Sprinkle the chopped tomatoes on top and dot with the butter. Cover and cook on high for 2½ hours until tender. Serve immediately with crusty bread.

Warm Chickpea Salad

SERVES 6

1¼ cups dried chickpeas (garbanzo beans), soaked in cold water overnight or for at least 5 hours, drained, and rinsed

1 cup pitted ripe black olives

4 scallions, finely chopped

fresh parsley sprigs, to garnish

crusty bread, to serve

Dressing

2 tablespoons red wine vinegar

2 tablespoons mixed chopped fresh herbs, such as parsley, rosemary, and thyme

3 garlic cloves, finely chopped

½ cup extra virgin olive oil

salt and pepper

Method

1 Put the chickpeas in a saucepan, cover with fresh water, and bring to a rapid boil for at least 10 minutes. Drain and rinse the beans, then put them in the slow cooker and add enough boiling water to cover. Cover and cook on low for 12 hours.

2 Drain well and transfer to a bowl. Stir in the olives and scallions.

3 To make the dressing, whisk together the vinegar, herbs, and garlic in a pitcher and season to taste with salt and pepper. Gradually whisk in the olive oil. Pour the dressing over the warm chickpeas and toss lightly to coat. Garnish with the parsley sprigs and serve warm with crusty bread.

73

Winter Vegetable Medley

SERVES 4

2 tablespoons sunflower oil

2 onions, peeled and chopped

3 carrots, chopped

3 parsnips, chopped

2 bunches celery, chopped

2 tablespoons chopped fresh parsley

1 tablespoon chopped fresh cilantro

1¼ cups vegetable stock

salt and pepper

Method

1 Heat the oil in a large, heavy saucepan. Add the onions and cook over medium heat, stirring occasionally, for 5 minutes, until softened. Add the carrots, parsnips, and celery and cook, stirring occasionally, for an additional 5 minutes. Stir in the herbs, season with salt and pepper, and pour in the stock. Bring to a boil.

2 Transfer the vegetable mixture to the slow cooker, cover, and cook on high for 3 hours, until tender. Taste and adjust the seasoning if necessary. Using a slotted spoon, transfer the vegetables to warm plates, then spoon over a little of the cooking liquid. Serve immediately.

Eggplant Cakes

SERVES 4

2 eggplants

3 tablespoons olive oil, plus extra
    for greasing

2 onions, finely chopped

2 red bell peppers, seeded
    and chopped

1 large tomato, peeled and chopped

1/3 cup milk

2 egg yolks

pinch of ground cinnamon

3/4 cup finely crushed crispbread

1 1/4 cups sour cream

salt and pepper

fresh flat-leaf parsley sprigs,
    to garnish

Method

1 Halve the eggplants and scoop out the flesh. Reserve the shells and dice the flesh. Heat the oil in a large, heavy skillet. Add the onions and cook over low heat for 5 minutes. Add the diced eggplants, red bell peppers, and tomato and cook, stirring occasionally, for 15–20 minutes, until all the vegetables are soft. Remove the skillet from the heat.

2 Transfer the mixture to a food processor or blender and process to a puree, then scrape into a bowl. Beat the milk, egg yolks, and cinnamon in a pitcher. Season, then stir into the vegetable puree.

3 Brush four ramekins (individual ceramic dishes) or custard cups with oil and sprinkle with enough of the crispbread crumbs to coat. Tip out any excess. Mix about three-quarters of the remaining crumbs into the vegetable puree. Slice the eggplant shells into strips and use them to line the ramekins, leaving the ends overlapping the rims. Spoon the filling into the ramekins, sprinkle with the remaining crumbs, and fold over the overlapping ends of the eggplant. Cover the ramekins with aluminum foil.

4 Stand the ramekins on a trivet in the slow cooker and pour in enough boiling water to come about one-third of the way up the sides of the ramekins. Cover and cook on high for 2 hours.

5 To make a sauce, lightly beat the sour cream and season. Lift the ramekins out of the slow cooker and remove the foil. Invert onto serving plates, garnish with parsley sprigs, and serve immediately with the sauce.

75

Stuffed Cabbage

SERVES 6

2 cups mixed nuts, finely ground

2 onions, finely chopped

1 garlic clove, finely chopped

2 celery stalks, finely chopped

1 cup shredded American cheese
or cheddar cheese

1 teaspoon finely chopped fresh
thyme

2 eggs

1 teaspoon yeast extract

12 large green cabbage leaves

Tomato sauce

2 tablespoons sunflower oil

2 onions, chopped

2 garlic cloves, finely chopped

28-ounce can diced tomatoes

2 tablespoons tomato paste

1 1/2 teaspoons sugar

1 bay leaf

salt and pepper

Method

1 To make the tomato sauce, heat the oil in a heavy saucepan. Add the onions and cook over medium heat, stirring occasionally, for 5 minutes, until softened. Stir in the garlic and cook for 1 minute, then add the tomatoes, tomato paste, sugar, and bay leaf. Season to taste with salt and pepper and bring to a boil. Reduce the heat and simmer gently for 20 minutes, until thickened.

2 Meanwhile, mix together the nuts, onions, garlic, celery, cheese, and thyme in a bowl. Lightly beat the eggs with the yeast extract in a pitcher, then stir into the nut mixture. Set aside.

3 Cut out the thick stem from the cabbage leaves. Blanch the leaves in a large saucepan of boiling water for 5 minutes, then drain and refresh under cold water. Pat dry with paper towels.

4 Place a little of the nut mixture on the base end of each cabbage leaf. Fold the sides over, then roll up to make a neat package.

5 Arrange the packages in the slow cooker, seam side down. Remove and discard the bay leaf from the tomato sauce and pour the sauce over the cabbage rolls. Cover and cook on low for 3–4 hours. Serve the cabbage rolls hot or cold.

76

Mixed Vegetable Casserole

SERVES 4

15–16-ounce can cannellini beans, drained and rinsed

14-ounce can artichoke hearts, drained

1 red bell pepper, seeded and sliced

4 small turnips, sliced

8 ounces baby spinach leaves, trimmed

6 fresh thyme sprigs

2 1/2 cups frozen baby fava beans

1 tablespoon olive oil

2 tablespoons butter

4 shallots, chopped

4 leeks, sliced

3 celery stalks, sliced

3 tablespoons all-purpose flour

1 cup dry white wine

2/3 cup vegetable stock

salt and pepper

Method

1 Put the cannellini beans, artichoke hearts, red bell pepper, turnips, spinach, and four of the thyme sprigs into the slow cooker.

2 Cook the fava beans in a small saucepan of lightly salted boiling water for 10 minutes.

3 Meanwhile, heat the oil and butter in a large skillet. Add the shallots, leeks, and celery and cook over low heat, stirring occasionally, for 5 minutes, until softened. Stir in the flour and cook, stirring thoroughly, for 1 minute. Gradually stir in the wine and stock and bring to a boil, stirring thoroughly. Season to taste with salt and pepper.

4 Transfer the contents of the skillet to the slow cooker. Drain the fava beans, rinse and drain again, then add to the slow cooker. Stir well, cover, and cook on low for 2 1/2–3 hours. Remove and discard the thyme sprigs. Transfer to warm serving dishes and garnish with the remaining thyme sprigs. Serve immediately.

77

Summer Vegetable Casserole

SERVES 4

4 potatoes, peeled and cubed

2 zucchini, cubed

2 red bell peppers, seeded and cubed

2 red onions, sliced

2 teaspoons mixed dried herbs

1 cup hot vegetable stock

salt and pepper

Method

1 Layer all the vegetables in the slow cooker, sprinkling with herbs and salt and pepper between the layers.

2 Pour over the stock. Cover and cook on low for 7 hours. Transfer to warm serving bowls and serve immediately.

78

Parsley Dumpling Stew

SERVES 6

1 large sweet potato, cut into chunks

2 onions, sliced

2 potatoes, cut into chunks

2 carrots, cut into chunks

2 celery stalks, sliced

2 zucchini, sliced

2 tablespoons tomato paste

2 1/2 cups hot vegetable stock

1 bay leaf

1 teaspoon ground coriander

1/2 teaspoon dried thyme

15-ounce can corn kernels, drained

salt and pepper

Parsley dumplings

1 2/3 cups all-purpose flour

2 1/2 teaspoons baking powder

3/4 teaspoon salt

1/2 cup vegetable shortening

2 tablespoons chopped fresh flat-
leaf parsley, plus extra sprigs
to garnish

about 1/2 cup milk

Method

1 Put the sweet potato, onions, potatoes, carrots, celery, and zucchini into the slow cooker. Stir the tomato paste into the stock and pour it over the vegetables. Add the bay leaf, coriander, and thyme and season to taste with salt and pepper. Cover and cook on low for 6 hours.

2 To make the dumplings, sift the flour with the baking powder and salt into a bowl and stir in the shortening and chopped parsley. Add just enough of the milk to make a firm but light dough. Knead lightly and shape into 12 small balls.

3 Stir the corn kernels into the mixture in the slow cooker and place the dumplings on top. Cook on high for 30 minutes. Transfer to warm serving plates, garnish with parsley sprigs, and serve immediately.

Spring Stew

SERVES 4

1 cup dried cannellini beans, soaked overnight or for at least 5 hours in cold water, drained, and rinsed

2 tablespoons olive oil

4–8 pearl onions, halved

2 celery stalks, cut into 1/4-inch slices

4 carrots, halved if large

8 new potatoes, halved

3 1/2–5 cups vegetable stock

1 bouquet garni (sprigs of parsley, bay leaf, and thyme tied together)

1 1/2–2 tablespoons light soy sauce

6 baby corns

3/4 cup fava beans, thawed if frozen

2 1/2 cups shredded cabbage

1 1/2 tablespoons cornstarch

salt and pepper

2/3–1 cups grated Parmesan-style vegetarian cheese, to serve

Method

1 Put the cannellini beans in a saucepan, cover with fresh water, and bring to a rapid boil for 10 minutes. Drain and rinse the beans again, then set aside.

2 Heat the oil in a saucepan. Add the onions, celery, carrots, and potatoes and cook over low heat, stirring frequently, for 5–8 minutes, until softened. Add the stock, cannellini beans, bouquet garni, and soy sauce, bring to a boil, then transfer to the slow cooker.

3 Add the baby corns, fava beans, and cabbage, season with salt and pepper, and stir well. Cover and cook on high for 3–4 hours, until the vegetables are tender.

4 Remove and discard the bouquet garni. Stir the cornstarch and 3 tablespoons of water to a paste in a small bowl, then stir into the stew. Re-cover and cook on high for an additional 15 minutes, until thickened. Serve the stew with the cheese.

Stuffed Bell Peppers

SERVES 4

1/2 cup long-grain rice

4 red bell peppers

15–16-ounce can chickpeas (garbanzo beans), drained

2/3 cup of canned or frozen corn kernels

4 scallions, sliced

1 tablespoon chopped fresh thyme

1 tablespoon olive oil

2/3 cup vegetable stock

salt and pepper

Method

1 Cook the rice in lightly salted, boiling water for 10 minutes, or according to the package directions, until almost tender. Drain well.

2 Slice the tops from the bell peppers and remove the seeds and membranes. Cut a small slice from the bottom of each so they sit firmly.

3 Mix together the rice, chickpeas, corn, scallions, thyme, oil, salt, and pepper. Spoon into the bell peppers and replace the lids.

4 Place the bell peppers in the slow cooker. Pour in the stock, cover, and cook on low for 5 hours, or until tender. Transfer to warm serving plates and serve immediately.

Baked Eggplant & Zucchini

SERVES 4

2 large eggplants

olive oil, for brushing

2 large zucchini, sliced

4 tomatoes, sliced

1 garlic clove, finely chopped

⅓ cup dry bread crumbs

3 tablespoons grated Parmesan-style vegetarian cheese

salt and pepper

basil leaves, to garnish

Method

1 Cut the eggplants into fairly thin slices and brush with oil. Heat a large, ridged grill pan or heavy skillet over high heat, then add the eggplants and cook in batches for 6–8 minutes, turning once, until soft and brown.

2 Layer the eggplants in the slow cooker with the zucchini, tomatoes, and garlic, seasoning with salt and pepper between the layers.

3 Mix the bread crumbs with the cheese and sprinkle over the vegetables. Cover and cook on low for 4 hours.

4 Transfer to warm serving bowls, garnish with basil leaves, and serve immediately.

Sweet & Sour Sicilian Pasta

SERVES 4

1/4 cup olive oil

1 large red onion, sliced

2 garlic cloves, finely chopped

2 red bell peppers, seeded and sliced

2 zucchini, cut into sticks

1 eggplant, cut into sticks

2 cups tomato puree

1/4 cup lemon juice

2 tablespoons balsamic vinegar

1/2 cup pitted ripe black olives, sliced

1 tablespoon sugar

14 ounces dried fettuccine

salt and pepper

fresh flat-leaf parsley sprigs,
   to garnish

Method

1 Heat the oil in a large, heavy saucepan. Add the onion, garlic, and bell peppers and cook over low heat, stirring occasionally, for 5 minutes. Add the zucchini and eggplant and cook, stirring occasionally, for an additional 5 minutes. Stir in the tomato puree and 2/3 cup of water and bring to a boil. Stir in the lemon juice, vinegar, olives, and sugar and season with salt and pepper.

2 Transfer the mixture to the slow cooker. Cover and cook on low for 5 hours, until all the vegetables are tender.

3 To cook the pasta, bring a large saucepan of lightly salted water to a boil. Add the fettuccine and bring back to a boil. Cook for 10–12 minutes, or according to the package directions, until the pasta is tender but still firm to the bite. Drain and transfer to a warm serving dish. Spoon the vegetable mixture over the pasta, toss lightly, garnish with parsley, and serve.

Vegetable Pasta

SERVES 4

9 ounces dried penne pasta

2 tablespoons olive oil, plus extra
for drizzling

1 red onion, sliced

2 zucchini, thinly sliced

3 cups sliced white button
mushrooms

2 tablespoons chopped
fresh oregano

3 small tomatoes, sliced

2/3 cup grated Parmesan-style
vegetarian cheese

salt and pepper

Method

1 Bring a large saucepan of lightly salted water to a boil. Add the pasta, bring back to a boil, and cook for 8–10 minutes, or according to the package directions, until tender but still firm to the bite. Drain. Meanwhile, heat the oil in a heavy saucepan, add the onions, and cook over medium heat, stirring occasionally, for 5 minutes, until softened. Stir into the pasta.

2 Place a layer of zucchini and mushrooms in the slow cooker and top with a layer of pasta. Sprinkle with oregano, salt, and pepper and continue layering, finishing with a layer of vegetables.

3 Arrange the sliced tomatoes on top and drizzle with oil. Cover and cook on high for 3 hours, or until tender.

4 Sprinkle with the grated cheese, cover, and cook for an additional 10 minutes. Transfer to a warm serving bowl and serve immediately.

Vegetable Curry

SERVES 4-6

2 tablespoons vegetable oil

1 teaspoon cumin seeds

1 onion, sliced

2 curry leaves

1-inch-piece fresh ginger, finely
chopped

2 fresh red chiles, seeded
and chopped

2 tablespoons Indian curry paste

2 carrots, sliced

1 cup snow peas

1 head of cauliflower, cut into florets

3 tomatoes, peeled and chopped

1/2 cup frozen peas, thawed

1/2 teaspoon ground turmeric

2/3–1 cup hot vegetable stock

salt and pepper

naan, to serve

Method

1 Heat the oil in a large, heavy saucepan. Add the cumin seeds and cook, stirring thoroughly, for 1–2 minutes, until they give off their aroma and begin to pop. Add the onion and curry leaves and cook, stirring occasionally, for 5 minutes, until the onion has softened. Add the ginger and chiles and cook, stirring occasionally, for 1 minute.

2 Stir in the curry paste and cook, stirring, for 2 minutes, then add the carrots, snow peas, and cauliflower. Cook for 5 minutes, then add the tomatoes, peas, and turmeric and season to taste with salt and pepper. Cook for 3 minutes, then add 2/3 cup of the stock and bring to a boil.

3 Transfer the mixture to the slow cooker. If the vegetables are not covered by the liquid, add more hot stock, then cover and cook on low for 5 hours, until tender. Remove and discard the curry leaves. Transfer to warm serving dishes and serve immediately with naan.

85

Vegetarian Paella

SERVES 6

1/4 cup olive oil

1 Bermuda onion, sliced

2 garlic cloves, finely chopped

4 cups hot vegetable stock

large pinch of saffron threads,
   lightly crushed

1 yellow bell pepper, seeded
   and sliced

1 red bell pepper, seeded and sliced

1 large eggplant, diced

1 1/4 cups paella or risotto rice

4 tomatoes, peeled and chopped

2 cups sliced cremini mushrooms

1 cup halved green beans

15–16-ounce can cranberry beans or
   pinto beans, drained and rinsed

salt and pepper

Method

1 Heat the oil in a large skillet. Add the onion and garlic and cook over low heat, stirring occasionally, for 5 minutes, until softened. Put 3 tablespoons of the hot stock into a small bowl and stir in the saffron, then set aside to steep.

2 Add the bell peppers and eggplant to the skillet and cook, stirring occasionally, for 5 minutes. Add the rice and cook, stirring thoroughly, for 1 minute, until the grains are coated with oil and glistening. Pour in the remaining stock and add the tomatoes, mushrooms, green beans, and cranberry beans. Stir in the saffron mixture and season to taste with salt and pepper.

3 Transfer the mixture to the slow cooker, cover, and cook on low for 2 1/2 –3 hours, until the rice is tender and the stock has been absorbed. Transfer to warm serving plates and serve immediately.

86

Mixed Bean Chili

SERVES 4–6

2/3 cup dried red kidney beans,
   soaked overnight or for at least
   5 hours, drained, and rinsed

2/3 cup dried black beans, soaked
   overnight or for at least 5 hours,
   drained, and rinsed

2/3 cup dried pinto beans, soaked
   overnight or for at least 5 hours,
   drained, and rinsed

2 tablespoons corn oil

1 onion, chopped

1 garlic clove, finely chopped

1 fresh red chile, seeded
   and chopped

1 yellow bell pepper, seeded
   and chopped

1 teaspoon ground cumin

1 tablespoon chili powder

4 cups vegetable stock

1 tablespoon sugar

salt and pepper

chopped fresh cilantro, to garnish

crusty bread, to serve

Method

1 Put the drained dried beans into a saucepan, cover with fresh water, and bring to a rapid boil for at least 10 minutes. Remove the pan from the heat, drain and rinse the beans, and set aside.

2 Heat the oil in a large heavy saucepan. Add the onion, garlic, chile, and yellow bell pepper and cook over medium heat, stirring occasionally, for 5 minutes. Stir in the cumin and chili powder and cook, stirring, for 1–2 minutes. Add the reserved beans and the stock and bring to a boil. Boil vigorously for 15 minutes.

3 Transfer the mixture to the slow cooker, cover, and cook on low for 10 hours, until the beans are tender.

4 Season to taste with salt and pepper, then ladle about one-third into a bowl. Mash well with a potato masher, then return the mashed beans to the slow cooker and stir in the sugar. Transfer to warm serving bowls and garnish with chopped cilantro. Serve immediately with crusty bread.

87

Spring Vegetable Risotto

SERVES 4

5 cups vegetable stock

large pinch of saffron threads

4 tablespoons (¼ stick) salted butter

1 tablespoon olive oil

1 onion, chopped

2 garlic cloves, finely chopped

1¼ cups risotto rice

3 tablespoons dry white wine

1 bay leaf

9 ounces young mixed vegetables, such as asparagus spears, green beans, baby carrots, baby fava beans and young green peas, thawed if frozen

2 tablespoons chopped flat-leaf parsley

⅔ cup grated Parmesan-style vegetarian cheese

salt and pepper

Method

1 Put ⅓ cup of the stock into a small bowl, crumble in the saffron threads, and let steep. Reserve ⅔ cup of the remaining stock and heat the remainder in a saucepan.

2 Meanwhile, melt half of the butter with the oil in a separate large saucepan. Add the onion and garlic and cook over low heat, stirring occasionally, for 5 minutes, until softened. Stir in the rice and cook, stirring thoroughly, for 1–2 minutes, until all the grains are coated and glistening. Pour in the wine and cook, stirring thoroughly, for a few minutes, until all the alcohol has evaporated. Season to taste with salt and pepper. Pour in the hot stock and the saffron mixture, add the bay leaf, and bring to a boil, stirring thoroughly.

3 Transfer the mixture to the slow cooker, cover, and cook on low for 2 hours. Meanwhile, if using fresh vegetables, slice the asparagus spears, green beans, and carrots and blanch all the vegetables in boiling water for 5 minutes. Drain and reserve.

4 Stir the reserved stock into the rice mixture, if it seems dry, and add the mixed vegetables, sprinkling them evenly over the top. Re-cover and cook on low for an additional 30–45 minutes, until heated through.

5 Remove and discard the bay leaf. Gently stir in the parsley, the remaining butter, and the cheese and serve immediately.

88

Asparagus & Spinach Risotto

SERVES 4

2 tablespoons olive oil

4 shallots, finely chopped

1 1/2 cups risotto rice

1 garlic clove, crushed

1/2 cup dry white wine

3 1/2 cups vegetable stock

8 ounces asparagus spears

8 ounces baby spinach leaves

1/2 cup grated Parmesan-style
  vegetarian cheese

salt and pepper

Method

1 Heat the oil in a skillet, add the shallots, and sauté over medium heat, stirring, for 2–3 minutes. Add the rice and garlic and cook for an additional 2 minutes, stirring. Add the wine and let boil for 30 seconds.

2 Transfer the rice mixture to the slow cooker, add the stock, and season to taste with salt and pepper. Cover and cook on high for 2 hours, or until most of the liquid is absorbed.

3 Cut the asparagus into 1 1/2-inch lengths. Stir into the rice, then spread the spinach over the top. Replace the lid and cook on high for an additional 30 minutes, until the asparagus is just tender and the spinach is wilted.

4 Stir in the spinach with the cheese, then adjust the seasoning to taste and serve immediately in warm bowls.

5

CAKES & DESSERTS

89

Chocolate Cake

SERVES 8

14 ounces semisweet dark chocolate

3/4 cup (1 1/2 sticks) unsalted butter,
  plus extra for greasing

3/4 cup firmly packed light
  brown sugar

4 eggs

2 teaspoons vanilla extract

1 1/4 cups all-purpose flour

1 3/4 teaspoons baking powder

1/2 teaspoon plus a pinch of salt

1/2 cup ground almonds

1/2 cup heavy cream

Method

1 Place a trivet or a ring of crumpled aluminum foil in the bottom of the slow cooker. Grease and line the bottom of a deep, 8-inch diameter cake pan, or a cake pan that fits into your slow cooker.

2 Melt 9 ounces of the chocolate in a bowl set over a saucepan of simmering water. Remove from the heat and cool slightly.

3 Beat the butter and sugar in a large bowl until pale and fluffy. Gradually beat in the eggs. Stir in the melted chocolate and 1 teaspoon vanilla of extract. Fold in the flour, baking powder, salt, and almonds evenly.

4 Spoon the batter into the prepared pan, spreading it evenly. Place in the slow cooker, cover, and cook on high for 2 1/2 hours or until risen and springy to the touch.

5 Remove from the slow cooker and let the cake rest in the pan for 10 minutes. Turn out and cool on a wire rack.

6 Place the remaining chocolate and vanilla extract in a saucepan with the cream and heat gently, stirring, until melted. Cool until thick enough to spread. Split the cake into two layers and sandwich together with the filling.

90

Chocolate & Walnut Sponge

SERVES 4–6

2/3 cup unsweetened cocoa powder,
plus extra for dusting

2 tablespoons milk

1 cup all-purpose flour

1 1/2 teaspoons baking powder

1/2 teaspoon salt

1/2 cup (1 stick) unsalted butter,
softened, plus extra for greasing

1/2 cup sugar

2 eggs, lightly beaten

1/2 cup chopped walnut pieces

whipped cream, to serve

Method

1 Grease a 1 1/4-quart casserole dish with butter. Cut out a double circle of wax paper that is 2 3/4 inches wider than the rim of the dish. Grease one side with butter and make a pleat in the center.

2 Mix the cocoa and milk to a paste in a small bowl. Sift the flour, baking powder, and salt into a separate small bowl. Set aside.

3 Beat together the butter and sugar in a large bowl until pale and fluffy. Gradually beat in the eggs, a little at a time, then gently fold in the sifted flour mixture, followed by the cocoa mixture and the walnuts.

4 Spoon the batter into the prepared dish. Cover the dish with the wax paper circles, buttered side down, and tie in place with string. Stand the dish on a trivet in the slow cooker and pour in enough boiling water to come about halfway up the side of the dish. Cover and cook on high for 3–3 1/2 hours.

5 Carefully remove the dish from the slow cooker and discard the wax paper. Run a knife around the inside of the dish, then turn out onto a warm serving dish. Serve immediately with whipped cream, dusted with cocoa.

91

Sponge Cake with Toffee Sauce

SERVES 6

1 cup chopped hazelnuts, toasted

1/2 cup (1 stick) unsalted butter, plus
  extra for greasing

1/2 cup firmly packed dark
  brown sugar

2 eggs, lightly beaten

1 cup all-purpose flour, sifted

1 1/2 teaspoons baking powder, sifted

1/2 teaspoon salt

1 tablespoon lemon juice

Caramel sauce

4 tablespoons unsalted butter

1/4 cup firmly packed dark
  brown sugar

1/4 cup heavy cream

1 tablespoon lemon juice

Method

1 Grease a 3 1/2-cup casserole dish with butter and sprinkle half of the nuts over the bottom. Cut out a double circle of wax paper that is 2 3/4 inches wider than the rim of the dish. Make a pleat in the center.

2 To make the caramel sauce, put the butter, sugar, cream, and lemon juice into a saucepan. Set the pan over low heat and stir until the mixture is smooth and thoroughly combined. Remove the pan from the heat. Pour half of the sauce into the prepared dish and swirl gently to coat part of the side. Reserve the remainder.

3 Beat together the butter and sugar in a bowl until light and fluffy. Gradually beat in the eggs, then gently fold in the flour, baking powder, salt, lemon juice, and the remaining hazelnuts. Spoon the batter into the dish. Cover the dish with the wax paper rounds and tie in place with string.

4 Stand the dish on a trivet in the slow cooker and pour in enough boiling water to come about halfway up the side of the dish. Cover and cook on high for 3–3 1/4 hours, until just set.

5 Shortly before serving, gently reheat the reserved caramel sauce. Carefully remove the dish from the slow cooker and discard the wax paper. Run a knife around the inside of the dish, then invert onto a warm serving dish. Serve with the reserved caramel sauce.

92

Lemon Sponge Cake

SERVES 4

3/4 cup granulated sugar

3 eggs, separated

1 1/4 cups milk

3 tablespoons self-rising flour, sifted

2/3 cup lemon juice

confectioners' sugar, for dusting

Method

1 Using an electric mixer, beat the granulated sugar with the egg yolks in a bowl. Gradually beat in the milk, followed by the flour and the lemon juice.

2 Whisk the egg whites in a separate grease-free bowl until stiff. Fold half of the whites into the yolk mixture using a plastic spatula in a figure-eight movement, then fold in the remainder. Try not to knock out the air.

3 Pour the batter into a heatproof dish and cover with aluminum foil. Stand the dish on a trivet in the slow cooker and pour in enough boiling water to come about one-third of the way up the side of the dish. Cover and cook on high for 2 1/2 hours, until the batter has set and the sauce and sponge have separated.

4 Carefully remove the dish from the slow cooker and discard the foil. Transfer to warm bowls, lightly dust with confectioners' sugar, and serve immediately.

Strawberry Cheesecake

SERVES 6–8

6 tablespoons unsalted butter,
   melted

1¼ cups crushed graham crackers

12 ounces strawberries

2½ cups cream cheese

1 cup sugar

2 extra-large eggs, beaten

2 tablespoons cornstarch

finely grated rind and juice
   of 1 lemon

Method

1 Place a trivet or a ring of crumpled aluminum foil in the bottom of the slow cooker. Stir the butter into the crushed crackers and press into the bottom of an 8-inch round springform pan, or a cake pan that fits into your slow cooker.

2 Puree or mash half of the strawberries and beat together with the cheese, sugar, eggs, cornstarch, and lemon rind and juice until smooth.

3 Transfer the mixture to the prepared pan and place in the slow cooker. Cover and cook on high for about 2 hours, or until almost set.

4 Turn off the slow cooker and let the cheesecake stand in the cooker for 2 hours. Remove and let cool completely, then carefully invert out of the pan.

5 Decorate with the remaining strawberries and serve.

Apple Crumble

SERVES 4

½ cup all-purpose flour

⅔ cup rolled oats

⅔ cup firmly packed light brown sugar

½ teaspoon freshly grated nutmeg

½ teaspoon ground cinnamon

½ cup (1 stick) unsalted butter, softened

4 cooking apples, such as Granny Smith, peeled, cored, and sliced

½–⅓ cup apple juice

Greek-style yogurt, to serve

Method

1 Sift the flour into a bowl and stir in the oats, sugar, nutmeg, and cinnamon. Add the butter and mix in with a pastry blender or the tines of a fork.

2 Place the apple slices in the bottom of the slow cooker and add the apple juice. Sprinkle the flour mixture evenly over them.

3 Cover and cook on low for 5½ hours. Serve hot, warm, or cold with yogurt.

Rice Pudding

SERVES 4

3/4 cup short-grain rice

4 cups milk

1/2 cup sugar

1 teaspoon vanilla extract

ground cinnamon,
* to decorate*

Method

1 Rinse the rice well under cold running water and drain thoroughly. Pour the milk into a large, heavy saucepan, add the sugar, and bring to a boil, stirring continuously. Sprinkle in the rice, stir well, and simmer gently for 10–15 minutes. Transfer the mixture to a heatproof dish and cover with aluminum foil.

2 Stand the dish on a trivet in the slow cooker and pour in enough boiling water to come about one-third of the way up the side of the dish. Cover and cook on high for 2 hours.

3 Remove the dish from the slow cooker and discard the foil. Stir the vanilla extract into the rice, then spoon it into warm bowls. Lightly dust with cinnamon and serve immediately.

96

Italian Bread Pudding

SERVES 6

unsalted butter, for greasing

6 slices panettone

3 tablespoons Marsala wine

1¼ cups milk

1¼ cups light cream

½ cup sugar

grated rind of ½ lemon

pinch of ground cinnamon

3 extra-large eggs, lightly beaten

Method

1 Grease a 1-quart casserole dish with butter. Place the panettone on a deep plate and sprinkle with the Marsala.

2 Pour the milk and cream into a saucepan and add the sugar, lemon rind, and cinnamon. Gradually bring to a boil over low heat, stirring until the sugar has dissolved. Remove the pan from the heat and let cool slightly, then pour the mixture onto the eggs, beating continuously.

3 Place the panettone in the prepared dish, pour in the egg mixture, and cover with aluminum foil. Stand the dish on a trivet in the slow cooker and pour in enough boiling water to come about one-third of the way up the side of the dish. Cover and cook on high for 2½ hours, until set.

4 Carefully remove the dish from the slow cooker and discard the foil. Let cool, then chill in the refrigerator until required. Run a knife around the inside of the dish, then invert onto a serving dish. Serve immediately.

97

Thai Black Rice Pudding

SERVES 4

1 cup black glutinous rice

*2 tablespoons firmly packed
   light brown sugar*

2 cups coconut milk

1 cup water

3 eggs

2 tablespoons sugar

Method

1 Mix together the rice, brown sugar, and half of the coconut milk in a saucepan, then stir in the water. Bring to a boil, then reduce the heat and simmer, stirring occasionally, for 15 minutes, until almost all the liquid has been absorbed. Transfer the mixture to a heatproof dish or ramekins (individual ceramic dishes).

2 Lightly beat the eggs with the remaining coconut milk and the sugar. Strain, then pour the mixture over the rice.

3 Cover the dish with aluminum foil. Stand the dish on a trivet in the slow cooker and pour in enough boiling water to come about one-third of the way up the side of the dish. Cover and cook on high for 2–2½ hours, until set. Carefully remove the dish from the slow cooker and discard the foil. Serve hot or cold.

Almond Charlotte Russe

SERVES 4

unsalted butter, for greasing

10–12 ladyfingers

1¼ cups milk

2 eggs

2 tablespoons sugar

½ cup chopped, blanched almonds

4–5 drops almond extract

Sherry sauce

1 tablespoon sugar

3 egg yolks

2/3 cup cream sherry

Method

1 Grease a 2½-cup ovenproof bowl with butter. Line the bowl with the ladyfingers, cutting them to fit and placing them cut sides down and sugar-coated sides outward. Cover the bottom of the bowl with some of the scrap pieces.

2 Pour the milk into a saucepan and bring just to a boil, then remove from the heat. Beat together the eggs and sugar in a heatproof bowl until combined, then stir in the milk. Stir in the almonds and almond extract.

3 Carefully pour the mixture into the prepared bowl, making sure that the ladyfingers stay in place, and cover with aluminum foil. Stand the bowl on a trivet in the slow cooker and pour in enough boiling water to come about halfway up the side of the bowl. Cover and cook on high for 3–3½ hours, until set.

4 Shortly before serving, make the sherry sauce. Put the sugar, egg yolks, and sherry into a heatproof bowl. Set the bowl over a saucepan of simmering water, without letting the bottom of the bowl touch the surface of the water. Whisk well until the mixture thickens, but do not let it boil. Remove from the heat.

5 Carefully remove the bowl from the slow cooker and discard the foil. Let stand for 2–3 minutes, then invert onto a warm serving plate. Pour the sherry sauce around it and serve immediately.

Crème Brûlée

SERVES 6

1 vanilla bean

4 cups heavy cream

6 egg yolks

1/2 cup granulated sugar

*1/3 cup firmly packed light
   brown sugar*

Method

1 Using a sharp knife, split the vanilla bean in half lengthwise, scrape the seeds into a saucepan, and add the bean. Pour in the cream and bring just to a boil, stirring continuously. Remove from the heat, cover, and let steep for 20 minutes.

2 Whisk together the egg yolks and granulated sugar in a bowl until thoroughly mixed. Remove and discard the vanilla bean, then whisk the cream into the egg yolk mixture. Strain the mixture into a large pitcher.

3 Divide the mixture among six ramekins (individual ceramic dishes) and cover each with aluminum foil. Stand the ramekins on a trivet in the slow cooker and pour in enough boiling water to come about halfway up the sides of the ramekins. Cover and cook on low for 3–3 1/2 hours, until just set. Remove the slow cooker pot from the base and let cool completely, then remove the ramekins and chill in the refrigerator for at least 4 hours.

4 Preheat the broiler to medium for 10 minutes. Sprinkle the brown sugar evenly over the surface of each dessert, then cook under the preheated broiler for 30–60 seconds, until the sugar has melted and caramelized. Alternatively, you can use a cook's blowtorch. Return the ramekins to the refrigerator and chill for an additional hour before serving.

100

Chocolate Desserts

SERVES 6

1¼ cups light cream

1¼ cups whole milk

8 ounces semisweet dark chocolate,
  broken into small pieces

1 extra-large egg

4 egg yolks

¼ cup sugar

⅔ cup heavy cream

chocolate curls, to decorate

Method

1 Pour the light cream and milk into a saucepan and add the chocolate. Set the pan over low heat and stir until the chocolate has melted and the mixture is smooth. Remove from the heat and let cool for 10 minutes.

2 Beat together the egg, egg yolks, and sugar in a bowl until combined. Gradually stir in the chocolate mixture until thoroughly blended, then strain into a pitcher.

3 Divide the mixture among six ramekins (individual ceramic dishes) and cover each with aluminum foil. Stand the ramekins on a trivet in the slow cooker and pour in enough boiling water to come about halfway up the sides of the ramekins. Cover and cook on low for 3–3½ hours, until just set. Remove the slow cooker pot from the base and let cool completely, then remove the ramekins and chill in the refrigerator for at least 4 hours.

4 Whip the heavy cream in a bowl until it holds soft peaks.
Top each chocolate dessert with a little of the whipped cream and decorate with chocolate curls. Serve immediately.